THE GREAT BRITISH
BAKING SHOW
Comfort Bakes

THE GREAT BRITISH
BAKING SHOW
Comfort
Bakes

SPHERE

CONTENTS

A note from Paul

Year on year, our bakers produce stand-out bakes that either become a particular new favourite for the judges or are a variation on a theme that gives us something original and special. Often, those exceptional bakes are the ones that the bakers have made with pure joy – a joy that translates to a well-executed recipe and great flavour. The common theme for many of those successes is that they are the bakes created with one extra ingredient – a happy memory that adds a sense of comfort and love to the result. This collection brings together some of the best examples of that.

Nothing beats the comforting aroma of home-baked cakes, breads and pastries filling your kitchen, and the anticipation of sharing those bakes with others, or tucking in as a treat for yourself. I believe that baking is in our DNA – so many memories contain shared experiences of bakes enjoyed with family, friends, neighbours and colleagues; so many textures and flavours feel like an extra wrapping of love when we're in need. I haven't met anyone who doesn't smile when remembering the delicious treats their grandma would bake for them, or that they baked together on rainy days. One bite has the ability to take us back to the joy of being five years old and presented with something sweet, delicious, homely and full of love. It's a gift that we pay forward, too; even if you don't already have that connection, you have an opportunity to be that someone for someone else. From friends and family to school fairs, fêtes and bake sales, you have a window to make not only your own, but someone else's day shine. Baking with comfort in mind gives you the opportunity to create your own homespun legacy. This book is filled with inspiration for just that.

A note from Prue

With the exception perhaps of a cup of tea or a bowl of soup, I think cake is *the* most comforting thing. And this book is all about delivering that cosy, comfy feeling you get when you eat a slice of cake, or bread still warm from the oven, or a baked pudding that just hits the spot. Many of the recipes in this book are easy to bake, not too time-consuming and above all familiar and delicious, but there's also comfort in tackling the more involved bakes – which fully immerse you in the process and, of course, wow your friends.

When I talk to the bakers, I'm always interested how many of them mention childhood treats that represent the comfort and love of home: a cake or biscuit after school; making cakes with a favourite nan; their mum's signature bake that appeared on high days and holidays. And is there anything in the world as comforting as the smell of baking bread? I don't think so, unless it is the feel of just-risen dough – smooth, tender and soft to the touch, like a baby's bum.

I know it doesn't work for everyone, but I find the act of baking, and indeed almost all cooking, comforting. Where other people will go for a walk in the park or countryside, or sink into a warm bath to soothe their woes, if I'm upset or anxious, my go-to remedy is the kitchen. As soon as I'm buried in a recipe, I forget whatever was bugging me, and my mood lifts. And when the cake comes out of the oven, there is no resisting a slice. I tell myself I deserve it, and it's better than gobbling a whole packet of chocolate digestives or a box of chocs.

This book, like all *Bake Off* books, aims to inspire. But this one has a special emphasis on bakes we find comforting: to make, to serve, and to eat. I hope you like it as much as I do.

Introduction

Welcome to the *Great British Bake Off: Comfort Bakes*, a collection of sweet and savoury bakes from Paul, Prue and the team behind the show, as well as, of course, the 2024 bakers themselves.

This year our book is all about comfort. Talking to our bakers and all the people involved in making our show, it's clear that in recent times, the notion of comfort has taken on a significance that extends beyond cosy socks, snuggly blankets and duvet days (although they are still important, too!). Instead, when the world seems out of kilter, comfort finds itself in unexpected spaces, not least at our kitchen table. It's in this vein that we have carefully curated all the recipes in this latest *Bake Off* book, in the hope that whatever 'comfort' or 'comfort bake' means to you, there will be plenty to feed your soul, as well as your sweet tooth.

What is comfort?

The ancient Greek philosopher and physician Hippocrates is credited with saying, 'Cure sometimes, treat often, comfort always', which seems a neat way to sum up the fact that no matter where we are or how we are feeling, our need for comfort is universal. Where medicine might not have the answer, the comfort of others – or comfort in whatever form it comes – can at least bring us a sense of peace, care and security.

But, how does that translate to baking? Ask yourself this: if you had to choose a single bake that most helped you feel contented, safe and at ease with yourself, what would it be? Perhaps you would choose a sumptuous piece of chocolate cake, like the one opposite (see recipe, page 189); or perhaps it would be an oaty biscuit (page 66) or a hearty curry pie (page 101) with all your favourite condiments; or perhaps you'd choose warm, crisp toast (page 72), dripping with melted butter and topped with sweet strawberry jam. Identifying your favourite comfort food, though, is likely to be the easy part. Once you've chosen it, ask yourself why? What is it about that particular bake that makes it your go-to when you need a little self-care?

For some of us, it will be because the bake evokes memories of times gone by. That oat cookie might have been the treat you had on your way home from school, or with a glass of milk before bedtime when you went for a sleepover at a favourite grandparent or aunt or uncle's house. The chocolate cake might be less about the nostalgia of the bake and more about its texture – a soft, tender crumb and decadent buttercream frosting that sticks to your fingers in lickable deliciousness. Perhaps the steaming pie with crisp, buttery pastry is about neither memory nor texture, and instead about what it means when you eat it – family or friends gathered together, with convivial laughter never far away. As soon as you begin to unpick where comfort comes from, you realise that comfort isn't one-dimensional and it doesn't mean one single thing, even to one single person. For all of us, comfort comes in many forms and for many reasons, and that's why choosing recipes for a book on comfort bakes has been fun and challenging in equal measure! We hope you love the results.

Using this book

Because every bake in the book might represent comfort in myriad ways to different people, we're leaving you to decide what bake will put the world to rights as the mood takes you. To that end, we have organised the book according to our most popular signature weeks: Cake, Biscuits, Bread, Pastry, Patisserie, Dessert, Chocolate and Free-from. Within each chapter you'll find comfort bakes that, in typical *Bake-Off* style, come with a modern twist. For example, Prue has reinvented her favourite apple tarte tatin into a version using sweet, caramelised pears (see page 137); Paul's signature loaf has become a seven-strand plaited wreath (page 86); and rather than offering a recipe for traditional jam tarts, we're taking all that's nostalgic about those treats and creating a gorgeous Italian-style crostata, instead (page 125). Among much more.

You might wonder how patisserie, with all its delicacy and intricate precision, can claim itself as comforting – but, in this case, we've selected bakes where the process itself becomes a mindful meditation with awesome results. The acts of laminating pastry, finely decorating a tart, and dipping madeleines in chocolate are themselves moments of comfort for those who need to take time out from their busy lives. Meanwhile, the 'big' bakes – among them, tiered cakes, pizza and family-sized pies – are here for gathering people together in the soothing cheer of togetherness; and the small bakes – from flapjacks to mini Victoria sponges and savoury biscuits for cheese – make for treats that are not only indulgent for one, but lovely for giving, to bring the gift of comfort to someone else in need.

The book finishes with 'Inspire Me', which reorganises all of our bakes in a more intuitive way – along the lines of how you might choose a bake to bring comfort to a particular mood or occasion. As always, there are no hard-and-fast rules – rather, in the hope of inspiring you, we've re-grouped all the recipes in the book into those for Duvet Days, Nostalgia, Sending Love, Rainy Days, Lose Yourself, Surrounded by Love and By the Fireside so that however you're seeking to give or receive comfort, an idea for a bake is at hand. And remember, very often, the comfort you're looking for lies not in the result, but in the time you give to the making itself.

Notes on the recipes

Oven temperatures: Ovens vary – not only from brand to brand, but from the front to the back of the oven, as well as (in a non-fan oven) between the top and bottom shelves. Invest in an oven thermometer if you can, which will give you a more accurate reading of the heat in your oven. Always preheat the oven, and use dry oven gloves.

Eggs: Eggs are medium and should be at room temperature, unless specified. Some recipes may contain raw or partially cooked eggs. Pregnant women, the elderly, babies and toddlers, and people who are unwell should be aware of these recipes.

Butter: In the recipes, 'softened butter' means to soften to room temperature, unless otherwise specified. 'Softened' means you should be able to leave an indentation with your fingertip when you press down.

Herbs, vegetables and fruit: Use fresh herbs and fresh, ripe, medium-sized vegetables and fruit unless the recipe specifies otherwise.

Spoon measures: All teaspoons and tablespoons are level unless otherwise stated.

Waxed citrus: When a recipe calls for citrus zest, it's preferable to use unwaxed fruit. However, some citrus, such as grapefruits and blood oranges, are hard to find unwaxed. In this case, before zesting, place the fruit in a colander, pour over boiling water, then dry the fruit thoroughly to remove the waxy residue.

Allergies or special diets: We want you to share these recipes with your loved ones and your community as often as possible. Please be aware, though, that some recipes contain allergens. If you are baking for others, do check before you share – there is a delicious collection of allergy-friendly recipes in the Free-from chapter on pages 213–235.

Andy
Essex
Car Mechanic

Family lies not only at the centre of Andy's world, but also of his baking. As a child, baking alongside his mum, Andy first learned the much-loved family staples: apple crumble to follow a Sunday roast and Bakewell tarts made using pastry offcuts (to make sure nothing went to waste) among them. Now, he bakes for his partner, Nickie, and hopes to inspire his daughter, Maisie, to follow in his baking footsteps – always with the aim of making his adored mum proud! When he's not in the kitchen, Andy is incredibly active. He plays football, goes to the gym and loves a long walk with Nickie, Maisie and their miniature Schnauzer, Arthur, as well as exploring the far corners of the country in their motor home.

Christiaan
London
Former Menswear Designer

Born in Emmen, a small town in The Netherlands, close to the border with Germany, Christiaan studied fashion in Amsterdam and then moved to the UK seven years ago, arriving in London to work for a leading fashion brand. He is passionate about visiting modern art galleries and stately homes. He loves nurturing his veg patch and dancing away in his kitchen to his favourite pop tunes! His eye for fashion and design is definitely something he brings to his bakes, which are meticulously detailed and beautiful, as well as his love of gardening – floral scents and citrus notes are among his favourite flavours. Bread is where he finds comfort – reminding him of the age-shaped bakes his mum would make for him and his siblings on their birthdays.

Dylan
Buckinghamshire
Retail Assistant

Curiosity for culture runs through Dylan's veins and he loves to travel. He recently took a gap year travelling through Southeast Asia, exploring the food and meeting new people at every stop. He is an avid skateboarder and has a fascination for the way that '90s PCs and vintage cars were built. With influence from his artistic mum, he has always loved to paint and will paint Japanese-inspired characters and cartoons on his t-shirts. Super-proud of his fusion roots – his mother is Indian and his father Japanese–Belgian – Dylan loves experimenting with sweet and spice in his baking. His presentation style is influenced by the beautiful Japanese bakes he tried on his travels and through following the work of French pâtissérie chefs on social media.

Georgie
Carmarthenshire
Paediatric Nurse

Georgie's love of food, and particularly of baking, is firmly embedded in her Italian roots and in the days she spent cooking with her Nonna Rosa. Georgie is a nature-loving forager, who takes inspiration from the food growing in the fields and hedgerows around her, as well as the abundance in her garden and the discoveries she has made on her travels. She is a self-proclaimed cannoli connoisseur! Along with a husband and three children at home in their Welsh farmhouse, Georgie has ten chickens, two ducks, two dogs and a cat. She has an impressive collection of crockery and tableware (to the point of obsession) and loves to sing in her kitchen – musicals, and especially *The Phantom of the Opera*, are a favourite.

Gill
Lancashire
Senior Category Manager

Gill is convinced that her love of precision data and her inherent creativity are the perfect match for successful baking. She can't remember a time when she didn't bake – growing up, baking was very much a family activity. Since her father passed away in 2015, Gill has used baking as a source of comfort and has put her skills to good use, raising money for Alzheimer's charities in his memory. Pies, cakes and pastry, including her dad's signature lemon meringue pie, were staples of her childhood, so her baking is very much traditional in style with a modern twist. Her sticky toffee Christmas pudding has been a hit at family celebrations for the past five years! Gill's claim to fame? In 1993 she was the UK's youngest ever driving instructor, aged 21.

Hazel
Kent
Former Nail Technician

Married to her childhood sweetheart for 51 years, Hazel has four children, one of whom still lives at home while the other three, and her ten grandchildren, all live close by. She loves nothing more than to gather everyone together for dinners and parties, and especially loves their get-togethers at Christmas. Ask Hazel to make you a birthday cake and it may well come with working parts – she has made several 'car' cakes with remote-controlled wheels and working lights. Her granddaughter's seventh birthday cake was a carousel with 500 edible diamonds that took Hazel two weeks to make! When she's not baking or entertaining her family, Hazel will be exercising her competitive streak, playing bingo.

Meet the bakers **13**

Illiyin
Norfolk
Birth Trauma Specialist Midwife

Born in London as one of eight siblings, Illiyin grew up in Norfolk in a busy household in which she helped her mum to bake, soon becoming the go-to family member for birthday cakes. Living in a community of myriad cultures and nationalities, Illiyin is inspired by the ingredients and flavours of many different cuisines. For example, she loves using Middle Eastern ingredients, such as dried fruits, nuts, honey, rose and mint, in her cakes; while her savoury bakes are typically inspired by the flavours of the Caribbean. A qualified midwife and published author, Illiyin now freelances to help women as they embark on their parenthood journey. She lives with her sister and nieces, and her Spanish husband and their two young children.

Jeff
West Yorkshire
Former University Lecturer

Originally from the Bronx, in New York, Jeff arrived in the UK in 1979, when he emigrated with his English girlfriend (now wife), whom he'd met while she was hitchhiking her way across America and he was a sports coach for a summer camp. They have lived in Yorkshire since 1987. A keen and competitive sportsman, Jeff has now hung up his basketball boots, but still loves swimming, going to the gym and long countryside walks. He began baking in earnest when his children were little, having learned the basics from his Hungarian grandmother and great-grandmother when he himself was a child. As you might hope (and perhaps even expect), he makes a mean New York Cheesecake.

John
West Midlands
Directorate Support Manager

Born and bred in the West Midlands, John has been a hairdresser and an estate agent, but he found his calling working in the NHS, keeping schedules and theatre bookings running like clockwork. His job keeps him busy, so after work his favourite pastime is to relax at home with his cockapoo, Stanley. Over weekends, you can find John and Stanley hitting the countryside for long walks. John learned to bake with his nan, making fairy cakes and pies, and now bakes to honour his nan's memory and pass on the skills she taught him to his two young nephews. He loves classic bakes with a twist – using herbs and other flavourings to give his bakes something different. His favourite bake, though, is a classic lemon tart.

Mike
Wiltshire
Farm Manager

Shortlisted for Young Farmer of the Year at the 2024 National Arable and Grassland Awards, and considered a friend to all, Mike is a fourth-generation farmer, working on his family farm alongside his parents and sister. He is an advocate for the LGBTQ+ community within farming and was an ambassador for the National Farmers Union in 2022. Amazingly, Mike is growing all the flowers for his upcoming wedding to partner Matt. Mike's baking style is homely and wholesome. He likes making big, hearty bakes using high-quality local ingredients that can satisfy lots of people at parties and gatherings. He especially loves using seasonal fruits and edible flowers from his garden and farm – and is even making his own wedding cake.

Nelly
Dorset
Palliative Care Assistant

Alongside her busy job in night-time palliative care, Nelly is a devoted mum to two young boys, who, with her husband Farhan, are the biggest fans of her bakes. Nelly grew up with her dad in Slovakia, then moved to Austria to study nursing. Her dad loved to bake bread, but wasn't keen on sweet baking, so it was only as an adult, after she had attempted a neighbour's gingerbread recipe, that Nelly extended her skills. Completely self-taught, Nelly loves adding the flavours of Slovakian cuisine into her bakes, as well as spices representing her husband's Pakistani heritage – apple and cinnamon are among her favourite ingredients. Nelly indulges her creative talents making jewellery, and is a big fan of true crime.

Sumayah
Lancashire
Dentistry Student

Presently on her gap year, Sumayah is indulging her sweet tooth before going onto study Dentistry. She lives in Lancashire with her parents and siblings and not only aced her sciences, but is incredibly creative, too – she is a keen sewer, making her own clothes, and has recently taken up photography. An entirely self-taught baker, Sumayah meticulously researches her creations, combining myriad techniques and recipes to create an eclectic and imaginative fusion of cultures and flavours. The project that confirmed her love for baking was a macaron tower she made for her aunt's mehndi wedding celebration – the result stood 1 metre tall, included 240 macarons in four different flavours, and a cascade of flowers.

Cake

Serves 16
Hands on 1½ hours
Bake 35 mins

For the stem ginger sponges
250g golden syrup
50g treacle
4 tbsp stem ginger syrup
190g dark muscovado sugar
190g salted butter
4 pieces of stem ginger, finely grated
375g self-raising flour
1 tbsp ground ginger
2 tsp mixed spice
1½ tsp bicarbonate of soda
3 large eggs
400ml whole milk

For the brown sugar buttercream
300g light brown soft sugar
6 large egg whites
500g salted butter, cubed and softened
20 drops cardamom extract (or the ground seeds of 30 cardamom pods)

For the honeycomb
½ tsp bicarbonate of soda
¼ tsp ground ginger
50g caster sugar
1½ tbsp golden syrup

To decorate
3 small figs, quartered
small handful of blackberries, halved if large

YOU WILL NEED
20cm solid-base round sandwich tins x 3, greased, then base-lined with baking paper
sugar thermometer
large piping bag fitted with a medium closed star nozzle
450g loaf tin or 15cm cake tin, greased, then lined (base and sides) with baking paper
silicone mat

Brown sugar and spice cake

Sugar and Spice and all things nice, that's what this cake is made of! This warming ginger and cardamom-spiced cake, with the crackle of honeycomb, conjures up all that is wonderful about a fireside. The sponges are surprisingly light for a sticky ginger cake and pair beautifully with the light cardamom Italian meringue buttercream.

1. Heat the oven to 180°C/160°C fan/Gas 4.

2. Make the stem ginger sponges. Heat the golden syrup, treacle, stem ginger syrup, dark muscovado and butter in a medium saucepan over a medium heat, stirring occasionally until the butter and sugar have melted. Stir in the grated stem ginger until it's evenly distributed, then remove the pan from the heat and set aside.

3. Sift the flour, ground spices and bicarbonate of soda into a large mixing bowl. Lightly whisk the eggs and milk together in a small jug.

4. Pour the warm syrup mixture over the dry ingredients and, using a balloon whisk, gently whisk together, until completely incorporated. Add the egg mixture and gently whisk until smooth and just combined.

5. Divide the mixture equally between the 3 lined tins. Bake for 25–30 minutes, until risen and a skewer inserted into the centres comes out clean. Remove from the oven and leave to cool in the tins for 5 minutes, before turning out onto a wire rack to cool completely.

6. Make the brown sugar buttercream. Meanwhile, tip the sugar into a medium saucepan, add 50ml of water and set over a high heat. Bring to the boil and boil until the sugar thermometer reads 115°C.

7. At this point, whisk the egg whites in the bowl of a stand mixer fitted with the whisk, until they reach stiff peaks.

8. When the temperature on the thermometer reaches 121°C, remove the pan from the heat and slowly pour the sugar syrup down the inside of the bowl, whisking continuously on a low speed. Increase the speed to medium and whisk to stiff peaks and the bowl is cool to the touch (about 5 minutes).

9. Gradually add the butter to the meringue, whisking continuously until smooth. Whisk in the cardamom extract. Spoon the buttercream into the piping bag fitted with the closed star nozzle.

Continues overleaf

10. Make the honeycomb. Stir the bicarbonate of soda and ground ginger together in a small bowl.

11. Tip the caster sugar and golden syrup into a deep saucepan set over a low heat, swirling the pan occasionally until the sugar has dissolved.

12. Increase the heat and boil until the mixture is a light golden caramel colour and the temperature on the sugar thermometer reaches 160°C (about 3–4 minutes). Immediately remove the pan from the heat and tip in the bicarbonate of soda and ginger, beating quickly but carefully with a wooden spoon until you can no longer see the powders. Pour the mixture into the lined loaf or cake tin and set aside for 30 minutes, or until the honeycomb has set firm. Once hardened, break the honeycomb into small pieces.

13. Assemble the cake. Pipe a dot of the buttercream in the centre of a cake plate or stand. Place one of the sponges on top and pipe swirls closely together around the edge and in the centre of the sponge, sprinkle one third of the honeycomb pieces over the buttercream.

14. Place a second sponge on top and repeat with the buttercream and another third of the honeycomb.

15. Sit the third sponge on top and pipe 4 generous swirls of buttercream in the centre of the sponge. Using an offset spatula, spread the buttercream evenly over the top. Pipe swirls of buttercream closely together around the edge.

16. Arrange the figs and blackberries in the centre of the cake. Using your hands, crush the remaining one third of honeycomb into small pieces and sprinkle over the top and sides to finish.

Serves 8–10
Hands on 40 mins
Bake 50 mins

240g unsalted butter,
    at room temperature
225g golden caster sugar,
    plus 1½ tbsp
500g rhubarb, trimmed
    and cut on the diagonal
    into 4cm slices
4 eggs, lightly beaten
1 tsp vanilla paste
finely grated zest of ¼ orange
200g plain flour
2½ tsp baking powder
50g ground almonds
1 tsp ground ginger
1 tsp ground cardamom
pinch of salt
2 tbsp soured cream
    or whole milk

For the custard
250ml whole milk
250ml double cream
1 vanilla pod, split and
    seeds scraped
3 egg yolks
1½ tbsp cornflour
50g caster sugar

YOU WILL NEED
23cm solid-base cake tin,
    greased, then base-lined
    with baking paper

Rhubarb upside-down cake with custard

Rhubarb and custard have made a winning combination in British desserts for more than 200 years. Soothe yourself with this classic cake, warm from the oven, with lashings of custard poured over.

1. Heat the oven to 180°C/160°C fan/Gas 4.

2. Prepare the filling. Spread 15g of the butter into the base of the cake tin on top of the baking paper and scatter with the 1½ tablespoons of caster sugar. Arrange the rhubarb, rounded side down, in a neat chevron pattern on top of the sugar.

3. Make the sponge. In a stand mixer fitted with the beater, beat the remaining 225g of butter and the 225g of caster sugar, on medium speed for 3–5 minutes, until pale and creamy, scraping down the inside of the bowl from time to time. Gradually add the beaten eggs, mixing well between each addition. Add the vanilla and orange zest and mix again.

4. Sift the flour, baking powder, ground almonds, ginger, cardamom and salt into the bowl. Add the soured cream or milk and mix again until the batter is smooth and thoroughly combined.

5. Carefully spoon the batter into the prepared tin on top of the rhubarb, spread it level and bake for 45–50 minutes, until well risen, golden brown and a skewer inserted into the centre comes out clean.

6. Make the custard. Towards the end of the baking time, heat the milk, cream and vanilla seeds in a heavy-based saucepan over a medium heat to just below boiling point. In a large bowl, whisk the egg yolks, cornflour and caster sugar together. Pour the warmed milk over the egg mixture, whisking continuously. Pour the mixture back into the pan and cook it over a very low heat, stirring continuously, for 3–4 minutes, until smooth and thick enough to coat the back of the spoon. Remove from the heat and set aside.

7. Leave the baked cake to rest in the tin for 2 minutes, then carefully turn it out onto a serving plate and leave to cool until warm. Serve warm with the custard for pouring over.

Makes 8 (32 bite-sized slices)
Hands on 1½ hours
Bake 30 mins

For the sponges
175g salted butter, softened
175g caster sugar
1 tsp almond extract
3 eggs
175g self-raising flour
pink food colouring

For the apricot jam
100g apricots, stoned weight,
   roughly chopped
100g jam sugar

For the buttercream
75g unsalted butter, softened
150g icing sugar, sifted

For the marzipan
300g ground almonds
150g icing sugar, sifted
150g caster sugar
4 tbsp pasteurised egg white
¼ tsp almond extract
yellow food colouring
granulated sugar, for rolling

YOU WILL NEED
30 x 17cm strip of 2-in-1
   baking paper and foil
17cm square cake tin,
   lightly greased
cooking thermometer

Paul's mini Battenbergs

*Squares of pink and cream nostalgia wrapped up in marzipan, the classic
Battenberg design is variously said to be based on the crest of the German
aristocratic family of the same name, or to represent each of Battenberg's
four sons, one of whom married Princess Victoria, granddaughter of Queen
Victoria, in 1884. At* Bake Off, *though, we simply think of it as the perfect
example of a teatime treat, and all the comfort that goes with it.*

1. Prepare the tin. Fold the strip of baking paper/foil in half and, holding
the folded edge, fold it over by 6.5cm, then open up the foil on either
side and re-crease the centre folds to make a standing divider. Place the
divider in the centre of the prepared tin to separate it into two halves.

2. Heat the oven to 180°C/160°C fan/Gas 4.

3. Make the sponges. Beat the butter, caster sugar and almond extract
in a stand mixer fitted with the beater, on medium speed for 3–5 minutes,
until pale and creamy. One at a time, add the eggs, also adding
1 tablespoon of the flour to prevent curdling, if necessary. Fold in the
remaining flour, then divide the mixture in half. Fold a few drops of pink
food colouring into one half to make the colour of strawberry ice-cream.

4. Spoon each sponge mixture into the tin: put the plain mixture on one
side of the divider and the pink mixture on the other. Level both with a
palette knife. Bake for 25–30 minutes, until well risen and golden brown,
and a skewer inserted into the centres comes out clean. Leave in the tin
to cool for 5 minutes, then turn out onto a wire rack to cool completely.

5. Make the jam. Place the apricots and sugar in a small, deep-sided
pan. Bring to the boil over a low heat and cook until the sugar dissolves,
crushing the apricots with a potato masher. Increase the heat to high and
boil for 4 minutes, until the temperature reaches 105°C on the cooking
thermometer. Remove the pan from the heat and pass the jam through
a metal sieve into a heatproof bowl. Leave to cool and set.

6. Make the buttercream. Using a wooden spoon or an electric hand
whisk, beat the butter and the icing sugar in a bowl until very pale,
fluffy and smooth. Set aside until ready to use.

7. Make the marzipan. Blitz the ground almonds, icing sugar and caster
sugar in a food processor. Add the egg white and almond extract, then
pulse to a smooth paste. Remove from the processor and knead in a very

Continues overleaf

small amount of yellow food colouring until the marzipan is a pastel yellow colour. Cover with a tea towel until ready to use.

8. Assemble the mini Battenbergs. Once the sponges are cool, slice each one lengthways into 4 equal, long strips. Turn each strip of sponge onto its side, then cut each sponge strip lengthways down the middle. You should end up with 8 long fingers of white sponge and 8 long fingers of pink sponge.

9. Lay all the sponge fingers, alternating white and pink, side-by-side and spread thinly with buttercream.

10. Lay 2 alternating strips of sponge side-by-side and another 2 on top of each other (so that the pink sits on top of the white, and the white sits on top of the pink), spreading all sides with buttercream to stick them together and give a chequerboard effect. Trim the ends, then cut into 8cm lengths.

11. Roll out the marzipan on a work surface lightly dusted with granulated sugar to about 3mm thick. Cut the marzipan into eight 18 x 8cm rectangles, re-rolling as necessary.

12. Brush a marzipan rectangle very thinly with the apricot jam. Place a mini cake onto the middle of the marzipan and wrap it around the cake, smoothing it over the sides so it is tightly wrapped. Turn the cake over so the marzipan seam is on the underside. Repeat with the remaining marzipan, jam and cakes until all eight are complete. To serve, slice each cake into quarters, to give bite-sized slices that are perfect for nibbling.

Serves 10
Hands on 1 hour + cooling
Bake 40 mins

For the lemon curd
3 eggs
150g caster sugar
finely grated zest and juice
    of 2 unwaxed lemons
75g unsalted butter, diced

For the sponges
225g unsalted butter,
    at room temperature
225g caster sugar
4 eggs, lightly beaten
200g plain flour
25g cornflour
1 tbsp baking powder
pinch of salt
finely grated zest and juice
    of 1 lemon
2 tbsp whole milk

For the meringue
1 egg white
pinch of salt
150g caster sugar
½ tsp cornflour
½ tsp white wine vinegar
    or lemon juice

For the filling
200ml double cream

YOU WILL NEED
20cm loose-bottomed round
    sandwich tins x 2, greased,
    then lined (base and sides)
    with baking paper

Lemon meringue cake

This cake has it all – buttery lemoniness in the sponge, crisp meringue, tangy curd and luscious whipped cream. And, best of all, you can serve it for afternoon tea as well as for dessert. You may have a little more lemon curd than you need, but any leftover is bonus deliciousness on toast or scones.

1. Make the lemon curd. Separate 2 of the eggs, then cover and chill the separated egg whites for making the meringue later.

2. In a heatproof bowl, combine the 2 egg yolks and the remaining whole egg. Add the caster sugar and whisk to combine. Add half the lemon zest to the egg yolks (reserve the remainder to use in the cake) and all the juice and whisk to combine.

3. Set the bowl over a pan of simmering water and cook the curd gently, whisking occasionally for about 15 minutes, until the curd thickens to thickly coat the back of a spoon. Gradually add the diced butter, stirring to melt it into the curd after each addition. Once all the butter has melted, strain the curd into a bowl, cover the surface with baking paper and leave to cool. Then, chill until needed.

4. Heat the oven to 180°C/160°C fan/Gas 4.

5. Make the sponges. In a stand mixer fitted with the beater, beat the butter and caster sugar, on medium speed for 3–5 minutes, until pale and creamy, scraping down the inside of the bowl from time to time. Gradually add the beaten eggs, mixing well between each addition and scraping down the inside of the bowl as necessary.

6. Sift the plain flour, cornflour, baking powder and pinch of salt into the bowl and mix until just combined. Add the reserved lemon zest (from the curd), as well as the additional lemon zest and juice, and the milk, and beat again for 30 seconds, until the mixture is silky smooth.

7. Divide the mixture equally between the prepared tins, spreading it level using an offset palette knife.

8. Make the meringue. Working quickly, whisk the reserved 2 egg whites (from the curd) plus the extra egg white with the pinch of salt in a stand mixer fitted with the whisk, on medium speed for about 3 minutes, until the meringue holds soft peaks.

Continues overleaf

9. Little by little, add the caster sugar, whisking well between each addition until the meringue is smooth, glossy and holds a firm peak.

10. In a small bowl combine the cornflour and vinegar or lemon juice and add this to the meringue. Whisk to combine.

11. Spoon the meringue equally on top of each sponge, leaving a 1cm border around each edge.

12. Bake the sponges. Bake the meringue-topped sponges for 5 minutes, then reduce the oven temperature to 170°C/150°C fan/Gas 3 and bake for a further 30–35 minutes, until risen, the meringue is golden and crisp and a skewer inserted into the centre of each sponge comes out clean.

13. Leave the sponges to cool in the tins for 3 minutes, then carefully remove them from the tins and leave them to cool on a wire rack.

14. Make the filling. While the sponges are cooling, whisk the double cream until it holds firm peaks. Lightly marble 3 tablespoons of the cold lemon curd through the whipped cream.

15. Assemble the cake. Once the sponges are cool, place one sponge layer, meringue side down, on a serving plate and top with the whipped cream. Spoon over 2 tablespoons of the lemon curd and top with the second cake layer, this time meringue side up. Chill for 20 minutes to allow the cream to firm up before serving.

Serves 8–10
Hands on 40 mins
Bake 35 mins

For the sponges
325g self-raising flour
½ tsp baking powder
½ tsp bicarbonate of soda
1 tsp ground cinnamon
½ tsp freshly grated nutmeg
½ tsp mixed spice
pinch of salt
200g light brown soft sugar
3 eggs, lightly beaten
250g carrots (about 4),
    coarsely grated
250ml sunflower oil
175g tinned pumpkin purée
finely grated zest of ½ orange
½ tsp vanilla paste

For the frosting
120g unsalted butter, softened
240g icing sugar, sifted
1 tsp vanilla paste
½–1 tsp ground cinnamon,
    to taste (optional)
240g full-fat cream cheese

YOU WILL NEED
20cm round sandwich tins x 2,
    greased, then base-lined
    with baking paper
large piping bag fitted with
    a medium open star nozzle

BAKER'S RECIPE

Carrot and pumpkin cake

I absolutely adore autumn; it's my favourite time of the year: crunchy leaves, knitted jumpers, pies and hot chocolates, and pumpkin – which is now also a favourite flavour for my favourite cake! An all-in-one cake, this is one of the easiest cakes you will ever make, and is super-moist, light, and bursting with all the cosiness of autumn.

1. Heat the oven to 190°C/170°C fan/Gas 5.

2. Make the sponges. Sift the flour, baking powder, bicarbonate of soda, cinnamon, nutmeg, mixed spice and salt in a large mixing bowl. Add the soft brown sugar and mix to combine.

3. Mix in the eggs, carrots, oil, pumpkin purée, orange zest and vanilla until thoroughly combined.

4. Divide the mixture equally between the lined tins and spread it level with a palette knife. Bake on the middle shelf for 30–35 minutes, until well risen, golden brown, and a skewer inserted into the centres comes out clean. Leave the sponges to cool for 10 minutes in the tin, then carefully turn them out onto a wire rack to cool completely.

5. Make the frosting. Beat the butter using an electric hand mixer (or in a stand mixer with the whisk) until smooth and fluffy. Add the icing sugar, vanilla and cinnamon (if using) and beat on a low speed until combined. Mix in the cream cheese until smooth. Turn the speed up and continue to mix until the frosting is stiff enough to hold a floppy peak. Scoop the frosting into the piping bag fitted with a medium open star nozzle.

6. Assemble the cake. Place one sponge on a serving plate and pipe half of the frosting over the top, making concentric circles of buttercream 'scallops' all the way to the centre, covering the entire surface.

7. Top with the second sponge and pipe the remaining cream frosting on top, again creating concentric circles of buttercream scallops to cover.

Serves 10–12
Hands on 2½ hours + chilling
Bake 25 mins

For the sponges
250g unsalted butter,
    softened
250g caster sugar
4 eggs, lightly beaten
4 tsp instant espresso
    powder, dissolved in
    2 tsp just-boiled water
250g self-raising flour
1 tsp baking powder
pinch of salt
50g walnuts, finely chopped
25g 70% dark chocolate,
    coarsely grated
2 tbsp soured cream

For the coffee syrup
½ tsp instant espresso powder
½ tsp vanilla paste
1 tbsp caster sugar
2 tbsp just-boiled water

For the frosting
325g caster sugar
5 egg whites
pinch of salt
25g 70% dark chocolate,
    broken into pieces
425g unsalted butter,
    cubed and softened
½ tsp vanilla paste
5 tsp instant espresso
    powder, dissolved in
    2 tsp just-boiled water
12 edible gold balls
edible gold or bronze
    sprinkles, to decorate

YOU WILL NEED
18cm round sandwich tins x 3,
    greased, then base-lined
    with baking paper
18cm round cake board
cake-decorating turntable
4 medium piping bags
2 medium open star nozzles
medium ribbon nozzle
small open star nozzle
small piping bag fitted with
    a small writing nozzle

Coffee and walnut Lambeth cake

Just when you thought coffee cake couldn't get any better... A showstopper of an indulgent treat for a morning spent with precious friends, this coffee cake is ramped up with Lambeth-style piped decoration to become a go-to option for a gathering that celebrates a special occasion, too.

1. Heat the oven to 180°C/160°C fan/Gas 4.

2. Make the sponges. Beat the butter and caster sugar in a stand mixer fitted with the beater, on medium speed for 3–5 minutes, until pale and creamy, scraping down the inside of the bowl from time to time. Gradually add the beaten eggs, mixing well between each addition. Add the coffee mixture and beat again to combine. Sift the flour, baking powder and salt into the bowl. Add the walnuts, grated chocolate and soured cream and mix again until smooth and thoroughly combined.

3. Divide the mixture equally between the lined cake tins and spread it level with a palette knife. Bake the sponges on the middle shelves for 22–25 minutes, until well risen, golden brown, and a skewer inserted into the centres comes out clean. Leave to cool.

4. Make the coffee syrup. Combine all the ingredients in a small bowl and stir to dissolve the coffee and sugar. Set aside until needed.

5. Make the frosting. Mix the sugar and egg whites in a large heatproof bowl. Add the salt and 1 tablespoon of water and set the bowl over a pan of barely simmering water. Using a balloon whisk, whisk continuously for about 6 minutes, until the sugar dissolves, the mixture is hot to the touch, and the glossy meringue just holds a ribbon trail when you lift the whisk. Quickly scoop the meringue into the bowl of the stand mixer and whisk for about 5 minutes, until cold and thickened.

6. Meanwhile, melt the chocolate in a heatproof bowl set over a pan of gently simmering water or in the microwave in short bursts.

7. Gradually add the butter to the cooled meringue, whisking continuously, on medium speed and scraping down the inside of the bowl from time to time. Once you have added all the butter and the mixture is silky smooth, divide it between 3 bowls: scoop 4–5 tablespoons into one bowl and

Continues overleaf

add the vanilla paste; scoop 4–5 tablespoons into another bowl and stir in the melted chocolate. Add the dissolved coffee powder to the remaining buttercream mixture and beat until smooth.

8. Assemble the cake. Place one sponge on the cake board and brush the top with some of the coffee syrup. Using a palette knife, spread 3 heaped tablespoons of the coffee buttercream over the top and top with the second sponge. Repeat this layering, ending with the third sponge.

9. Place the cake on the cake-decorating turntable. Using a palette knife, spread a thin layer of coffee buttercream over the top and sides of the cake, to crumb coat. Chill for 30 minutes, until firm.

10. Decorate the cake. Return the cake to the turntable and cover the top and sides in a second smooth layer of coffee buttercream. Spoon half of the remaining coffee buttercream into a piping bag fitted with a medium open star nozzle and the remainder into a piping bag fitted with a ribbon nozzle. Spoon the vanilla buttercream into another piping bag, this time fitted with the small star nozzle. Scoop 2 tablespoons of the chocolate buttercream into the small piping bag fitted with the writing nozzle, and scoop the remainder into the final medium piping bag fitted with the other medium open star nozzle.

11. Place the cake on a serving plate and place the plate on the turntable. Pipe scallops of chocolate buttercream around the bottom edge of the cake and embellish with small vanilla rosettes.

12. Pipe 12 downward-pointing coffee scallops evenly spaced around the top of the side of the cake and pipe a vanilla rosette onto the pointed end of each. Decorate each rosette with an edible gold ball.

13. Using the coffee buttercream and ribbon nozzle, pipe ruffles around the top edge of the cake and chocolate rosettes in a circle inside this. Pipe more small vanilla rosettes in between the coffee and chocolate rings. Finally, using the small piping bag of chocolate buttercream, pipe chocolate 'ropes' between each scallop to join them around the top of the side of the cake.

14. Scatter the top of the cake with gold or bronze edible sprinkles and chill for 30 minutes before serving.

Serves 12
Hands on 2 hours + chilling
Bake 40 mins

For the pistachio sponges
150g unsalted butter, softened
175g caster sugar
1 egg, lightly beaten
3 egg whites
1 tsp vanilla paste
½ tsp almond extract
½ tsp green food-colouring
  paste
50g unsalted shelled
  pistachios
150g plain flour
25g cornflour
2 tsp baking powder
pinch of salt
2 tbsp whole milk,
  at room temperature

For the vanilla sponges
175g unsalted butter, softened
175g caster sugar
3 eggs, lightly beaten
2 tsp vanilla paste
150g plain flour
25g cornflour
2 tsp baking powder
pinch of salt
2 tbsp whole milk,
  at room temperature

For the filling and frosting
250g raspberries,
  plus extra to decorate
juice of ¼ lemon
500g caster sugar
1 tbsp vanilla paste
3 tbsp hot water
6 egg whites
pinch of salt
540g unsalted butter, softened
5 tsp freeze-dried
  raspberry powder
pink food-colouring paste

To decorate
50g unsalted shelled
  pistachios, finely chopped
edible fresh flowers

Continues overleaf

pistachio, raspberry and vanilla cake

This cake is pure, summery joy for a birthday or occasion – it's the kind of cake that makes everyone go 'ooh' as you bring it to the table. And it needn't even feel stressful to pull together – you can make the layers of sponge in advance, leaving just the buttercream, assembly and simple decoration for the morning, ahead of your party.

1. Heat the oven to 180°C/160°C fan/Gas 4.

2. Make the pistachio sponges. Beat the butter and caster sugar in a stand mixer fitted with the beater, on medium speed for about 3–5 minutes, scraping down the inside of the bowl from time to time, until pale and creamy. Add the beaten egg and beat well, then gradually add the egg whites, beating well between each addition. Add the vanilla, almond extract and green food-colouring paste and mix to combine.

3. Grind the pistachios in a food processor until very finely chopped and tip them into the bowl with the sponge mixture. Sift in the flour, cornflour, baking powder and salt, then add the milk and beat until smooth and combined.

4. Divide the mixture equally between the lined tins and spread it level with a palette knife. Bake on the middle shelf for about 20 minutes, until well-risen, golden brown, and a skewer inserted into the centre of each sponge comes out clean. Leave the sponges to cool in the tins for 2–3 minutes, then turn them out onto a wire rack to cool completely. Wash and dry the tins, then grease and re-line them.

5. Make the vanilla sponges. Beat the butter and caster sugar in a stand mixer fitted with the beater, on medium speed for about 3–5 minutes, scraping down the inside of the bowl from time to time, until pale and creamy. Gradually add the eggs, beating well between each addition. Add the vanilla and mix to combine. Sift the flour, cornflour, baking powder and salt into the bowl. Add the milk and beat until smooth and combined.

6. Divide the mixture equally between the lined tins and spread it level with a palette knife. Bake on the middle shelf for about 20 minutes, until well-risen, golden brown, and a skewer inserted into the centre of each sponge comes out clean. Leave the sponges to cool in the tins for 2–3 minutes, then turn them out onto a wire rack to cool completely.

Continues overleaf

pistachio, raspberry and vanilla cake (continued)

YOU WILL NEED
18cm round cake tins x 2, greased, then base-lined with baking paper
18cm round cake board
2 medium piping bags fitted with medium plain nozzles
cake scraper or offset palette knife
cake-decorating turntable (optional)
3 medium piping bags, each fitted with an open star nozzle of different size

7. Make the filling and frosting. Combine the raspberries, lemon juice and 50g of the caster sugar in a small saucepan and cook over a medium–low heat for about 5 minutes, crushing the berries with the back of a spoon, until the mixture is jammy. Pass it through a sieve to remove any seeds and leave to cool. This is your raspberry purée.

8. Combine 1 tablespoon of the raspberry purée, 50g of the remaining caster sugar, 1 teaspoon of the vanilla and the hot water in a small bowl. Mix to dissolve the sugar and create a syrup, and set aside.

9. Tip the remaining 400g of caster sugar into a large heatproof mixing bowl. Add the egg whites, salt and 1 tablespoon of water. Set the bowl over a pan of gently simmering water and whisk for about 7 minutes, until the sugar dissolves, the meringue has doubled in volume and is hot to the touch. Carefully remove the bowl from the heat, scoop the meringue into a stand mixer fitted with the whisk and whisk for about 7 minutes, until cold.

10. One tablespoon at a time, add the butter to the egg-white mixture, whisking well between each addition, to create a smooth buttercream. Whisk in the remaining vanilla.

11. Scoop half of the buttercream into a bowl. Add the remaining cooled raspberry purée and 3 teaspoons of the freeze-dried raspberry powder and mix to combine to an even pink. Scoop 3 tablespoons of the pink buttercream into a small bowl, cover and set aside for decorating the cake later.

12. Weigh out 100g of the remaining vanilla buttercream, cover and set it aside. Scoop the rest of the vanilla buttercream into a medium piping bag with a plain nozzle.

13. Assemble the cake. Lay the sponges on your work surface and, using a long-bladed serrated cake or bread knife, level the top of each one.

14. Place one pistachio sponge on the cake board and brush the top of the cake with raspberry syrup. Pipe a ring of vanilla buttercream around the edge of the first sponge. Spoon 100g of pink raspberry buttercream into the centre of the vanilla ring and spread it level.

15. Place a vanilla sponge on top, brush it with raspberry syrup and spread it with the reserved 100g of vanilla buttercream. Top with a pistachio sponge and repeat the previous decoration – pipe a ring of vanilla around the edge of the sponge and fill with pink raspberry buttercream. Top with the remaining vanilla sponge. Gently press the sponge layers together and chill for 30 minutes.

16. Place the cake on the cake-decorating turntable, if you have one. Using the cake scraper or palette knife, cover the top and sides of the cake with a very thin layer of vanilla buttercream from the piping bag, to create a crumb coat. Return the cake to the fridge for 20 minutes.

17. Divide the remaining raspberry buttercream equally between two bowls. Add a drop of pink food colouring to one bowl along with the remaining 2 teaspoons of freeze-dried raspberry powder and mix to combine. Scoop this buttercream into the second piping bag with a medium plain nozzle. Set the cake on the turntable and pipe raspberry buttercream rings around the cake, from the bottom of the cake to one-third of the way up the side.

18. Add 3 tablespoons of the remaining vanilla buttercream in the piping bag to the second bowl of raspberry buttercream to lighten the colour. Scoop this into the same piping bag and pipe further rings around the cake, from immediately above the last darker-pink ring to two-thirds of the way up the side.

19. Using the remaining vanilla buttercream, pipe further rings from immediately above the last pink ring to the top of the cake.

20. Using a palette knife, lightly smudge the different shades of buttercream together turning the cake on the turntable, to smooth the sides of the cake. The different-coloured rings of buttercream should lightly mix as you turn and smooth it, giving an ombre effect.

21. Cover the top of the cake in a smooth layer of the remaining vanilla buttercream from the piping bag.

22. Place the cake on a serving plate and press the chopped pistachios all around the bottom edge to create a skirt. Scoop any remaining buttercream plus the reserved 3 tablespoons of raspberry buttercream into the three piping bags, each with a different-sized star nozzle, and pipe decorative rosettes on the top of the cake. Decorate with edible flowers and scatter with a few raspberries, to serve.

Serves 16
Hands on 30 mins + soaking
Bake 40 mins

For the fruit
75g raisins
75g sultanas
75g pitted dried apricots,
    chopped into small pieces
75g pitted soft dates,
    chopped into small pieces
25g crystallised ginger,
    finely chopped
finely grated zest of ½ large
    orange, plus the juice of
    the whole

For the sponge
225g unsalted butter, softened
125g light muscovado sugar
100g golden caster sugar
1 tbsp treacle
3 eggs, lightly beaten
225g plain flour
2 tsp baking powder
1 tsp mixed spice
pinch of salt
2 tbsp whole milk
3 tbsp pearl or demerara sugar

YOU WILL NEED
20 x 30cm traybake tin,
    greased, then lined
    (base and sides)
    with baking paper

Fruit slice traybake

Soft, spicy and warming, with a satisfying crunch in the sugary top, these neat rectangles of fruit cake are all you need alongside a cup of tea, a book, and an afternoon all to yourself.

1. Prepare the fruit. Tip the raisins and sultanas into a small saucepan. Add the apricots, dates and crystallised ginger with the orange zest and juice and set the pan over a low heat to warm the juice, but do not boil. Remove the pan from the heat, mix well and leave for 30 minutes to allow the fruit to plump in the hot juice.

2. Heat the oven to 170°C/150°C fan/Gas 3.

3. Make the sponge. Beat the butter with both sugars in a stand mixer fitted with a beater, on medium speed for 3–5 minutes, scraping down the inside of the bowl from time to time, until pale and creamy. Add the treacle and mix again to combine.

4. Gradually add the beaten eggs, mixing well in between each addition. Sift in the flour, baking powder, mixed spice and pinch of salt, add the milk and mix on low speed until almost smooth.

5. Add the plumped fruit mixture, including the soaking juices, to the bowl and use a rubber spatula to combine.

6. Spoon the mixture into the prepared tin and spread it level. Scatter with the pearl or demerara sugar and bake for 35–40 minutes, until the cake is golden brown, well risen and a skewer inserted into the centre comes out clean.

7. Leave the cake to cool in the tin, then remove it and cut it into bars or slices to serve.

Serves 10
Hands on 1 hour
+ cooling and chilling
Bake 20 mins

For the genoise sponges
8 eggs
225g caster sugar
2 tsp vanilla extract
100g unsalted butter
140g plain flour
55g cocoa powder
10g cornflour

For the filling and frosting
650g mascarpone
200g icing sugar, sifted
1 tbsp vanilla paste
400ml double cream
1 tbsp light brown soft sugar
150ml strong espresso, cooled
3 tbsp cocoa powder,
    for dusting

YOU WILL NEED
20cm, deep round cake tins
    x 2, greased, then base-lined
    with baking paper
20cm, deep cake ring or
    deep tin, base-lined with
    baking paper and sides
    lined with acetate
medium piping bag fitted with
    a medium open star nozzle

Mochamisu layer cake

*This was the first bake I ever made for my family – a beautiful, big sharing
dessert, perfect for communal eating that ticks all the boxes. Enjoy!*

1. Heat the oven to 180°C/160°C fan/Gas 4.

2. Make the genoise sponges. Whisk the eggs and sugar in a stand
mixer fitted with a whisk, on medium speed for about 4 minutes, until
pale and doubled in size, and the mixture holds a firm ribbon trail
when you lift the whisk. Add the vanilla and whisk again to combine.

3. Melt the butter in a small saucepan and leave to cool slightly.

4. Sift the flour, cocoa and cornflour into the egg mixture and fold them
in with a large metal spoon or rubber spatula. Mix a large spoonful of
the mixture into the melted butter in the pan, then fold the contents
of the pan into the cake mixture until combined. Divide the mixture
equally between the lined cake tins and level with a palette knife.

5. Bake the sponges on the middle shelf for about 20 minutes, until
well risen, golden brown, and the centres spring back when pressed.
Leave to cool in the tins for 10 minutes, then turn out onto a wire rack
to cool completely. Once cooled, trim the domed top off each sponge,
if necessary, then slice each through the middle to create 4 equal layers.

6. Make the filling. Beat the mascarpone and icing sugar in a stand mixer
fitted with the beater, on low speed until smooth. Beat in the vanilla and
cream until it holds soft peaks. Meanwhile, stir the brown sugar into the
espresso until it dissolves.

7. Assemble the cake. Place 1 sponge layer in the bottom of the lined cake
ring or tin and brush with the cooled espresso. Add 4 heaped tablespoons
of the cream mixture, spread them level and dust the top with cocoa, sifting
it through a small sieve. Repeat the layering of the sponge, coffee, cream
and cocoa, ending with the fourth sponge layer. Cover the remaining
cream with foil and chill both cream and cake for 30 minutes.

8. Remove the cake from the fridge. Place a serving plate on top of the
cake ring, then flip it over and carefully remove the tin and acetate. Spoon
one quarter of the remaining cream into the piping bag fitted with an open
star nozzle and set aside. Using the leftover cream, decorate the top and
sides of the cake, spreading it over neatly with a palette knife. Pipe a ring
of rosettes around the top edge of the cake and return the cake to the
fridge for at least 3 hours, but up to 24 hours, to firm up. Lightly dust
with cocoa to serve.

Makes: 12
Hands on: 40 mins
Bake: 20 mins

For the sponges
150g unsalted butter,
  softened
150g caster sugar
1 tsp vanilla paste
3 eggs, lightly beaten
150g plain flour
15g cornflour
1½ tsp baking powder
pinch of salt
2 tbsp soured cream

For the filling
200ml double cream
1 tbsp icing sugar, sifted,
  plus extra for dusting
1 tsp vanilla paste
2 tbsp elderflower cordial
3 tbsp strawberry jam
12 fresh strawberries, hulled,
  9 thinly sliced, 3 quartered

YOU WILL NEED
12-hole mini Victoria sponge
  tin or a muffin tin, greased,
  then each hollow base-lined
  with a disc of buttered
  baking paper
piping bag fitted with a
  medium star nozzle

Mini Victoria sandwiches

A Victoria sandwich all to yourself – what could be lovelier? These are gorgeous to package into little boxes and deliver to friends who need to feel special.

1. Heat the oven to 180°C/160°C fan/Gas 4.

2. Make the sponges. Using a stand mixer fitted with the beater, beat the butter, caster sugar and vanilla, on medium speed for 3–5 minutes, until very pale and creamy. Gradually add the beaten eggs, mixing well between each addition.

3. Sift the flour, cornflour, baking powder and pinch of salt into the bowl. Add the soured cream and mix again on low speed until smooth.

4. Divide the batter equally between the hollows in the prepared tin and bake for about 20 minutes, until the sponges are well risen and golden, and a skewer inserted in the centre of each comes out clean. Cool the sponges in the tins for 2 minutes, then transfer them to a wire rack to cool completely.

5. Make the filling. Whisk the cream with the icing sugar, vanilla paste and elderflower cordial until it just holds a peak. Scoop the cream into the piping bag with a medium star nozzle. Set aside.

6. Assemble the cakes. Cut each sponge in half horizontally and spread the bottom halves with jam. Cover the jam with 2 strawberry slices, then pipe a swirl of cream on top of the strawberries and gently press the sponge tops into the cream (any leftover strawberry slices are cook's perks).

7. Dust the tops of the cakes with icing sugar, pipe with a cream rosette and finish with a quartered strawberry on each cake.

Biscuits

150g soft pitted dates,
   chopped into 1cm pieces
200g unsalted butter, diced
150g light brown soft sugar
125g golden syrup
50g date syrup
pinch of salt
200g rolled oats
200g porridge oats
75g pistachios,
   finely chopped
50g coconut chips,
   roughly chopped
35g sesame seeds

YOU WILL NEED
20 x 30cm brownie tin,
   greased, then lined
   (base and sides)
   with baking paper

Date and pistachio flapjacks

Any treat that poses as a healthy snack is a winner in our book! These flapjacks are next level – soft and fudgy and dotted with pistachios and dates to make them sumptuous, crunchy and sweet through and through.

1. Heat the oven to 190°C/170°C fan/Gas 5.

2. Tip the dates into a medium saucepan with 4 tablespoons of water. Place the pan over a medium–low heat and cook for about 5 minutes, mashing with a wooden spoon until the dates are very soft.

3. Add the butter, sugar, golden and date syrups and pinch of salt and continue to cook, stirring often, until the butter has melted and the sugar dissolved (about 3–4 minutes). Stir the mixture until it's smooth, then remove the pan from the heat.

4. Meanwhile, in a large mixing bowl combine the rolled and porridge oats, then add the pistachios, coconut chips and sesame seeds. Mix everything together to combine.

5. Add the butter and syrup mixture to the bowl and stir well. Tip the mixture into the lined brownie tin and use the back of a spoon to press it out into an even, firm layer.

6. Bake the flapjack for 25 minutes, until golden brown. Leave to cool completely in the tin before cutting into 16–20 equal squares or bars to serve. The flapjacks will keep for up to 7 days in an airtight container.

Makes 20
Hands on 30 mins
+ cooling and chilling
Bake 14 mins per batch

250g unsalted butter
200g light brown soft sugar
100g caster sugar
2 eggs, lightly beaten
325g plain flour
20g milk powder
1 tsp baking powder
1 tsp ground cinnamon
2 tsp instant espresso powder
¼ tsp salt
175g dark chocolate,
    roughly chopped into
    irregular 1.5cm pieces
100g milk chocolate,
    roughly chopped into
    irregular 1.5cm pieces

YOU WILL NEED
3 baking sheets, each lined
    with baking paper

BAKER'S RECIPE

Brown butter, coffee and cinnamon chocolate chip cookies

Who doesn't love a chocolate chip cookie?! They were the first thing I ever baked – and I used to take them into school to share with friends, or enjoy them at home with a glass of milk (another one of my favourite things). These are my grown-up version. I love the combination of coffee and cinnamon – adding chocolate makes them even more delicious.

1. Make the dough. Melt the butter in a pan over a medium–low heat for 3–5 minutes, until the milk solids separate and the butter is browned and has a nutty aroma. Remove the pan from the heat and pour the browned butter into the bowl of a stand mixer fitted with a beater, then leave to cool. Chill in the fridge to solidify (about 20 minutes).

2. Once the butter is solid, add both sugars to the mixer bowl and beat, on medium speed for about 2 minutes, until light and creamy. Gradually add the eggs, beating well between each addition. Scrape down the inside of the bowl as necessary.

3. Sift the flour, milk powder, baking powder, cinnamon, espresso powder and salt into the bowl and mix on low speed until incorporated. Fold in the pieces of dark and milk chocolate until evenly distributed.

4. Cover the bowl and leave the dough to rest in the fridge for a minimum of 2 hours, or preferably overnight. When you're ready to bake, heat the oven to 180°C/160°C fan/Gas 4.

5. Shape and bake the cookies. Shape the dough into 50g balls (it should make about 20 cookies) and place the balls on the lined baking trays, leaving space between them for them to spread (you should get about 7 on a tray).

6. Bake the cookies in batches for about 14 minutes per batch, until golden brown at the edges. Leave to cool for 5 minutes on the tray, then transfer to a wire rack to cool completely while you bake the remainder. The cookies will keep for up to 3 days in an airtight container.

Makes 16–18
Hands on 40 mins + chilling
Bake 16 mins

For the biscuits
220g unsalted butter,
    well softened
75g icing sugar, sifted
1 tsp vanilla paste
230g plain flour
30g cornflour
¼ tsp baking powder
pinch of salt

For the Irish cream filling
150g unsalted butter, softened
320g icing sugar
½ tsp vanilla paste
2 tsp cocoa powder
2 tbsp Irish cream liqueur

To decorate
100g 70% dark chocolate,
    broken into pieces
50g white chocolate,
    broken into pieces

YOU WILL NEED
large piping bag fitted with
    a large open star nozzle
2 baking sheets, each lined
    with baking paper
medium piping bag fitted with
    a medium open star nozzle
small freezer or piping bag

Boozy Viennese fingers

Homemade biscuits are among the loveliest gifts you can offer to a friend or neighbour, or even bring to a dinner party to thank your host. The Irish cream liqueur filling in these makes them extra-decadent.

1. Make the biscuits. Tip the butter into the bowl of a stand mixer fitted with the beater. Add the icing sugar and beat on medium speed for about 3 minutes, until really pale, soft and light. Add the vanilla and mix again to combine.

2. Sift the flour, cornflour, baking powder and salt into the bowl and mix on low speed until smooth and thoroughly combined.

3. Spoon the mixture into the large piping bag fitted with the large star nozzle and pipe equally sized 6–7cm fingers on the prepared baking sheets, leaving a little space between each one. Chill for 30–60 minutes.

4. Meanwhile, heat the oven to 170°C/150°C fan/Gas 3.

5. Bake the biscuits for about 16 minutes, until firm and just starting to turn golden at the edges. Leave to cool on the baking sheets for 3 minutes, then transfer them to a wire rack to cool completely.

6. Make the Irish cream filling. Beat the butter and icing sugar in a stand mixer fitted with the beater, on medium speed for 2–3 minutes, until really pale and creamy. Add the vanilla, cocoa and Irish cream liqueur and mix again to combine. Set aside.

7. Assemble and decorate the Viennese fingers. Melt the dark chocolate in a heatproof bowl over a pan of barely simmering water and stir until smooth. Dip one end of each biscuit into the melted dark chocolate and leave to set on a clean sheet of baking paper.

8. Melt the white chocolate in a heatproof bowl over a pan of simmering water and stir until smooth. Add 1 tablespoon of melted white chocolate to the liqueur buttercream, stir to combine, then spoon the buttercream into the medium piping bag fitted with the star nozzle. Set aside.

9. Scoop the remaining melted white chocolate into a small freezer or piping bag. Snip the corner into a fine point and drizzle it over the chocolate-coated ends of the biscuits. Leave to set.

10. Turn half of the biscuits flat side uppermost and pipe them with the liqueur buttercream. Sandwich with an identical biscuit, turning if necessary so that the chocolate coating is at the opposite end, top and bottom. The biscuits will keep in an airtight container for up to 3 days.

85g butterscotch candies
50g pecans
200g unsalted butter,
    softened
100g caster sugar,
    plus extra for sprinkling
1 tsp vanilla paste
250g plain flour
25g cornflour
25g rice flour
¼ tsp baking powder
pinch of salt

YOU WILL NEED
2 baking sheets, each lined
    with baking paper

Butterscotch and pecan shortbread biscuits

Shortbread (surely, the ultimate dunker?) has that melt-in-the mouth butteriness that is irresistibly moreish. We've added flecks of butterscotch and pecan to these – tiny pockets of chewy sweetness, along with a nutty crunch, to make them satisfying in every way.

1. Make the shortbread dough. Chop the butterscotch candies and pecans into small pieces – about half the size of a pea.

2. In the bowl of a stand mixer fitted with the beater, cream together the butter, caster sugar and vanilla, on medium speed for about 3 minutes, until pale and creamy.

3. Scrape down the inside of the bowl, then sift in the flour, cornflour, rice flour, baking powder and salt and mix until almost combined. Add the chopped butterscotch and pecans and mix slowly until the pieces are evenly distributed.

4. Turn out the mixture onto a lightly floured work surface and divide it in half. Shape each half into a 5–6cm-diameter log. Wrap the logs tightly in baking paper, twist the ends to seal and roll the logs back and forth on the work surface to neaten. Chill for 2 hours, until very firm.

5. Heat the oven to 170°C/150°C fan/Gas 3.

6. Bake the biscuits. Unwrap the shortbread logs and, using a sharp knife, cut them into 1cm-thick discs. Arrange the discs on the lined baking sheets, leaving a little space in between each disc.

7. Sprinkle the top of the shortbreads with a little caster sugar and bake for 12–13 minutes, until firm and starting to turn golden at the edges.

8. If any nuggets of butterscotch have escaped from the sides of the baked shortbreads, gently push them back into shape with a palette knife while the biscuits are still hot. Leave the biscuits to cool on the baking sheets for 5 minutes, then transfer them to a wire rack until cold. The shortbreads will keep for up to 7 days in an airtight container.

Makes 12
Hands on 1½ hours
+ chilling and freezing
Bake 25 mins

**For the shortbread
biscuit base**
120g unsalted butter,
    at room temperature
60g caster sugar
120g plain flour
60g rice flour
¼ tsp fine salt

For the mint fondant
50g white chocolate,
    broken into pieces
50g unsalted butter,
    at room temperature
100g icing sugar, sifted
1 tsp peppermint extract

For the chocolate coating
210g 54% dark chocolate,
    broken into pieces

To decorate
50g milk chocolate,
    broken into pieces

YOU WILL NEED
5cm plain round cutter
2 baking sheets, each lined
    with baking paper
3cm plain round cutter
cooking thermometer
small piping bag fitted with
    a small plain writing nozzle
green foil wrappers (optional)

Prue's mint chocolate biscuits

*The acts of unpeeling the green foil wrappers and biting through the layers
of chocolate, mint and biscuit feel like a rite of passage when it comes to
breaktime snacks. These home-baked versions of the classic lunchbox treat
come with a snappy shortbread base, fondant mint centre and crisp
chocolate coating. How will you eat yours?*

1. Make the shortbread biscuit base. Beat the butter and caster sugar
in a stand mixer fitted with the beater, on medium speed for 3 minutes,
until combined and soft but not aerated.

2. Add both flours and the salt and mix until the dough starts to clump
together, taking care not to overmix. Tip the dough onto the work surface
and use your hands to bring it together into a ball.

3. Place the dough between 2 sheets of non-stick baking paper and roll
it out to 1cm thick. Transfer the dough sheet (still between the sheets
of baking paper) to a baking sheet and chill it for 30 minutes.

4. Make the mint fondant. While the dough is chilling, melt the white
chocolate in a heatproof bowl set over a pan of gently simmering water,
stirring until smooth. Remove from the heat and transfer the chocolate to
a clean bowl, then leave to cool. Heat the oven to 160°C/140°C fan/Gas 3.

5. Beat the butter and icing sugar for the fondant in a stand mixer fitted
with the beater, on medium speed for 2–3 minutes, until smooth and
pale. Mix in the cooled white chocolate, then the peppermint extract.
Spoon the mixture onto a sheet of baking paper and, using a palette
knife, spread it out to a rectangle, about 20 x 7cm. Lift the baking
paper onto a baking sheet and freeze for 30 minutes.

6. Shape the biscuits. Using a 5cm round cutter, stamp out 12 rounds
from the chilled biscuit dough, re-rolling the trimmings if necessary.
Place them on one of the lined baking sheets and bake for 25 minutes,
until crisp and light golden. Remove from the oven and leave to cool on
the tray for 5 minutes, then transfer to a wire rack to cool completely.

7. Remove the fondant from the freezer and, using a 3cm round cutter,
stamp out 12 rounds of peppermint fondant and set these aside at
room temperature until needed.

Continues overleaf

8. Make the chocolate coating. Melt 140g of the dark chocolate in a heatproof bowl set over a pan of gently simmering water until it reaches 44°C on the cooking thermometer. Remove the bowl from the heat and add the remaining 70g of dark chocolate, stirring until it melts and cools to 32°C.

9. Assemble the biscuits. Dip the base of the cooled shortbread biscuits into the tempered dark chocolate and place them chocolate side-up on the other lined baking sheet. Chill for 15 minutes, until set, then place chocolate side-down on a wire rack set over a sheet of baking paper.

10. Place a disc of peppermint fondant in the centre of each biscuit on the cooling rack, then spoon the tempered chocolate over the top to cover the filling and exposed shortbread edge. Leave the chocolate to set slightly.

11. To decorate, melt the milk chocolate in a heatproof bowl set over a pan of gently simmering water, stirring until smooth. Remove the bowl from the heat and leave the chocolate to cool. Spoon the chocolate into the small piping bag fitted with the small, plain writing nozzle. Pipe thin lines backwards and forwards across each biscuit, then leave to set. Wrap the biscuits in green foil for a fully nostalgic option, if you wish. Either way, they will store in an airtight tin for up to 3 days.

Makes 16–20
Hands on 2 hours + setting + chilling
Bake 12 minutes

For the biscuits
200g plain flour
½ tsp baking powder
1 tsp ground ginger
1 tsp ground cinnamon
pinch of salt
100g unsalted butter,
    diced and chilled
75g light brown soft sugar
1 tsp finely grated
    unwaxed lemon zest
2 tbsp golden syrup
1 egg yolk
1 tsp lemon juice

For the icing
500g icing sugar,
    plus extra if needed
2 egg whites
red, yellow and black
    food-colouring pastes

YOU WILL NEED
6–8cm heart cutter
6–8cm plain round cutter
2 baking sheets, each lined
    with baking paper
4 small piping bags

Iced bug biscuits

These ingenious biscuits make the most of simple heart and round cutters to create fun insect shapes. They are the perfect rainy-day activity with the kids – why not use assorted-sized cutters to make a whole family of bugs?

1. Make the biscuits. Sift the flour, baking powder, ginger, cinnamon and salt into a mixing bowl or food processor. Rub in the butter with your fingertips, or use the pulse button, until the mixture starts to look like sand and only very small flecks of butter are still visible. Mix in the sugar and lemon zest to combine.

2. In a small bowl, combine the golden syrup with the egg yolk and lemon juice, then mix this into the biscuit mixture with a spatula until it starts to clump together. Tip out the dough onto the work surface and lightly knead it to bring it together into a smooth ball. Flatten the ball into a disc, cover and chill for 2 hours, until firm.

3. Roll out the dough on a lightly floured work surface until it is about 3mm thick. Using the cutters, stamp out heart and round shapes and arrange them slightly spaced apart on the lined baking sheets. Re-roll the trimmings and stamp out more shapes until you have used all the dough. Chill the dough shapes for 30 minutes.

4. Meanwhile, heat the oven to 180°C/160°C fan/Gas 4.

5. Bake the biscuits. Transfer the trays to the oven and bake for about 12 minutes, until the biscuits are lightly browned at the edges. Leave them to cool and firm up for about 5 minutes on the baking sheets, then transfer to a wire rack to cool completely.

6. Make the icing. Sift the icing sugar into a mixing bowl and beat in the egg whites with a balloon whisk for about 2 minutes, until smooth and thick. The icing should hold a ribbon trail for 5 seconds when the whisk is lifted from the bowl (you may need to add a little more cold water or icing sugar to achieve the required consistency).

7. Spoon 2 tablespoons of the icing into a small piping bag and tie a knot or use a food-bag clip to close the end and seal, then set aside. Divide the remaining icing between 3 bowls and tint one red, one yellow and one black using the food-colouring pastes. Spoon 2 tablespoons of each colour into separate piping bags, secure the open ends as before, and cover the remaining icing in the bowls.

Continues overleaf

8. Decorate the biscuits. For the bees, snip the end of the piping bag of black icing to a fine point and pipe an outline of the bee body on one half of each heart biscuit (use the photo to guide you) and leave the outline to dry for 30 minutes.

9. Meanwhile, for the ladybirds, snip the end of the piping bag of red icing to a fine point and pipe a fine line around the outside edge of each round biscuit. Leave to dry for 30 minutes.

10. Add a few drops of water to the yellow icing in the bowl to loosen slightly. When the black icing outlining the bee shape has set, spoon the yellow within the border to fill the shape and create a body. Leave to set for 2 hours, until firm.

11. Repeat with the red icing in the bowl inside the red outline on the round biscuits to make the ladybird bodies. Leave to set.

12. Snip the end of the piping bag of white icing into a fine point and pipe 2 wings and an eye onto each bee – you can do this simply by piping a heart shape over the empty part of the biscuit, then piping a line from the dip in the top of the heart shape to the point (to create the impression of two wings), then cross-hatching white icing in each part to create wing details. Pipe 5 curved black lines across each yellow bee body to make the outline for the stripes. Leave to set for 30 minutes.

13. Using the photo as a guide, pipe a black segment-shaped outline on top of the red of each ladybird biscuit for the head and 2 wings on the body section, then add the spots. Leave to set for 30 minutes.

14. Add a drop of water to the black icing in the bowl to loosen, then spoon it between the alternate lines on the bee bodies to fill in the stripes. Give each bee a smile, then add a dot of white icing for an eye. Leave to set for 10 minutes.

15. Pipe 2 white eyes onto each head segment of the ladybirds and leave to set for 10 minutes.

16. Add a dot of black icing to the eyes on both the bees and ladybirds and leave to set firm before serving. The biscuits will keep in an airtight container for up to 3 days.

Makes 40
Hands on 30 mins
Bake 14 mins

For the dough
250g plain flour
80g caster sugar
125g unsalted butter, softened
2 large egg yolks (reserve the
    whites for the meringue)
1 tsp vanilla extract

For the nutty meringue
2 large egg whites
125g caster sugar
100g walnuts, finely ground

To decorate
40 walnut halves

YOU WILL NEED
large piping bag fitted with
    a medium plain nozzle
5cm plain round cutter
2 baking sheets, each lined
    with baking paper

Hunters' Buttons

My super-super-favourite baking of all is making Christmas biscuits. In Slovakia, where I come from, Christmas officially begins on 5th December – and you know it because suddenly the shops sell out of spices and nuts and everywhere you go the air is filled with the scent of vanilla and cinnamon. There are so many Christmas biscuits that I love, but Hunters' Buttons are the ones that most remind me of home. They have a very delicate shortbread biscuit, topped with meringue and half a walnut. Delicious.

1. Make the dough. Sift the flour and sugar into a large mixing bowl or a stand mixer fitted with a beater. Add the butter, egg yolks and vanilla and beat until the mixture comes together into a smooth dough. Shape the dough into a disc, cover and chill for 15 minutes.

2. Make the meringue. While the dough is chilling, whisk the egg whites in the stand mixer (clean it first) fitted with the whisk, on medium speed for 3–4 minutes, until they hold soft peaks. A tablespoon at a time, add the sugar until the meringue is smooth, glossy and holds medium–firm peaks. Gently fold in the ground walnuts, then scoop the mixture into the piping bag fitted with a medium plain nozzle.

3. Heat the oven to 180°C/160°C fan/Gas 4.

4. Assemble and bake the biscuits. Lightly dust the work surface with flour and roll out the dough until about 4mm thick. Using the 5cm round cutter, stamp out the biscuits, arranging them slightly spaced apart on the lined baking sheets. Re-roll the trimmings and stamp out more biscuits until you have used all the dough – you should get about 40 biscuits altogether.

5. Pipe a neat mound of meringue to cover the top of each biscuit and place a halved walnut on top.

6. Bake for 12–14 minutes, until lightly browned at the edges and the meringue is crisp. Leave the biscuits to cool and firm up for 5 minutes on the baking sheets, then transfer to a wire rack to cool completely. The biscuits will keep in an airtight container for up to 3 days.

Makes 20
Hands on 30 mins
Bake 13 mins

175g unsalted butter, diced
125g golden syrup
1 tbsp tahini
1 tbsp boiling water
1 tsp bicarbonate of soda
175g plain flour, sifted
200g porridge oats
   (not rolled oats)
50g desiccated coconut
100g light brown soft sugar
pinch of salt

YOU WILL NEED
2 baking sheets, each lined
   with baking paper

Golden syrup cookies

These are a twist on the cookies of your childhood – the ones you were handed with a glass of milk as you stepped into the hallway and dropped your school bag by the door. We've added tahini to give a subtle nuttiness.

1. Heat the oven to 170°C/150°C fan/Gas 3.

2. Melt the butter in a small saucepan over a medium–low heat. Continue cooking until the butter starts to foam and the milk solids turn golden brown (about 3 minutes) – swirl the pan regularly so that the butter browns evenly.

3. Slide the pan off the heat, add the golden syrup, tahini, boiling water and bicarbonate of soda and stir to combine.

4. Combine the flour, porridge oats, coconut, sugar and salt in a mixing bowl. Add the butter mixture and mix until thoroughly combined.

5. Roll the mixture into walnut-sized balls. Arrange them on the lined baking sheets, spacing them well apart to allow for spreading.

6. Bake the cookies for about 12 minutes, until golden brown, then leave them to cool on the baking sheets for 5 minutes before transferring them to a wire rack to cool completely. The cookies will keep in an airtight container for 7 days.

Makes 40
Hands on 30 mins
+ cooling and freezing
Bake 35 mins + 15 mins
per batch

50g blanched hazelnuts
50g dried cranberries,
   roughly chopped
50g dried soft figs,
   roughly chopped
50g pumpkin seeds
50g sunflower seeds
1 tbsp poppy seeds
200g plain flour
125g spelt flour
½ tsp bicarbonate of soda
good pinch of sea-salt flakes
good grinding of black pepper
30g light brown soft sugar
250ml buttermilk
4 tbsp extra-virgin olive oil
1 tbsp runny honey

YOU WILL NEED
450g loaf tins x 2, greased,
   then lined (base and ends)
   with a strip of baking paper
2 baking sheets, each lined
   with baking paper

Fruit and nut crackers

*A cross between savoury biscotti and melba toast, these wafers are
intended for topping with hunks of your favourite cheese. With a glass
of wine in the other hand, they make for an easy fireside supper.
Alternatively, wrap them up and tie them with a ribbon for gifting
at a relaxed lunch with friends.*

1. Heat the oven to 180°C/160°C fan/Gas 4.

2. Tip the hazelnuts onto a baking tray and lightly toast in the oven
for 4 minutes, until pale golden. Very roughly chop the hazelnuts and
tip them into a mixing bowl with the cranberries, figs, and pumpkin,
sunflower and poppy seeds.

3. Sift both flours, the bicarbonate of soda, salt and pepper into the
mixing bowl. Add the sugar and mix to combine.

4. In a jug, mix the buttermilk, olive oil and honey together and add
the mixture to the dry ingredients. Mix well until combined, then use
your hands to very lightly knead the dough to bring it together until
almost smooth.

5. Divide the mixture in half and press each half into an even layer
in a lined tin. Bake for 30–35 minutes, until risen, firm and golden.
Remove the tins from the oven and leave the baked loaves to cool for
3–4 minutes, then turn them out onto a wire rack to cool completely.

6. Tightly wrap the loaves in foil and freeze them for 4–6 hours.

7. When you're ready to finish baking, heat the oven to 150°C/
130°C fan/Gas 2.

8. Using a serrated bread knife, cut the frozen loaves into wafer-thin
slices (about 2mm thick; you should get about 40 crackers altogether),
and arrange the slices in a single layer on the lined baking sheets.

9. Bake the wafers in batches for about 15 minutes per batch, swapping
the trays around and flipping the wafers over halfway through baking,
so that they bake evenly. They should be crisp and very lightly toasted.

10. Leave the crackers to cool on wire racks before serving, or storing
in an airtight box for up to 2 weeks.

Bread

Makes 1 loaf
Hands on 20 mins + rising
Bake 30 mins

500g strong white bread flour,
     plus extra for kneading
7g fast-action dried yeast
2 tsp salt
175ml buttermilk
175ml hot water
1 tsp runny honey
sunflower oil, for greasing
1 tbsp whole milk
1 tbsp poppy seeds

YOU WILL NEED
baking sheet lined
     with baking paper

Seeded bloomer

*Is there anything more homely than a bouncy, soft loaf with a crisp crust?
The smell of it baking alone is enough. The bloomer is the bake that keeps
on giving: warm toast (shiny with melted butter and slathered with jam
or marmalade); chunky bacon sandwiches; finger slices, thickly buttered
for dunking into warm soup or a dippy egg... We rest our case.*

1. Make the dough. Combine the flour, yeast and salt in the bowl of a
stand mixer fitted with a dough hook. Combine the buttermilk, hot water
and honey in a jug and pour the mixture into the bowl. With the mixer
on low speed, mix to combine with the dry ingredients.

2. Scrape down the inside of the mixer bowl, increase the speed to
medium and knead for 6–8 minutes, until the dough is smooth and
cleanly leaves the sides of the bowl.

3. Turn out the dough onto a clean work surface, lightly brush the bowl
with the oil, and shape the dough into a neat ball. Return the dough to
the bowl, then cover and leave at room temperature to rise for about
1 hour, or until doubled in size.

4. Shape the loaf. Turn out the dough onto a lightly floured work
surface and knead for 20 seconds to knock it back. Pat the dough into
a 20 x 30cm rectangle with a short side nearest to you. Fold the sides
in to the middle and roll the dough away from you in a tight spiral.

5. Place the rolled dough, seam-side down, on the lined baking sheet
and tuck the ends under to neaten. Using a sharp knife or lame, cut
6–8 diagonal slashes in the top of the loaf, cover loosely with a tea towel
and leave the shaped loaf to rise at room temperature for 45 minutes
to 1 hour, or until doubled in size and the dough slowly springs back
when gently pressed with a floured finger.

6. Heat the oven to 210°C/190°C fan/Gas 6–7 and place a small roasting
tin in the bottom of the oven at the same time.

7. Bake the loaf. Brush the loaf with the milk and scatter it with the poppy
seeds. Pour a mugful of water into the hot roasting tin in the oven and
transfer the loaf to the middle shelf. Bake for 30 minutes, until the bread
is golden brown, well risen and the underside sounds hollow when
tapped. Leave to cool completely on a wire rack before slicing.

Makes 12
Hands on 1 hour + rising
Cook 25 mins

For the doughnuts
500g strong white bread flour
75g caster sugar
7g fast-action dried yeast
1 tsp salt
225ml whole milk, lukewarm
2 eggs, lightly beaten
1 tsp vanilla paste
50g unsalted butter,
    cubed and softened
finely grated zest of
    ½ unwaxed orange
about 1½ litres sunflower oil,
    for deep-frying

For the crème filling
150g caster sugar
200ml double cream
20g unsalted butter
good pinch of sea-salt flakes
400ml whole milk
½ vanilla pod, split lengthways
4 egg yolks
30g cornflour
finely grated zest of
    ½ unwaxed orange

For the coating
250g caster sugar

For the glaze
75g 70% dark chocolate,
    broken into pieces
75g 54% dark chocolate,
    broken into pieces
40g unsalted butter, diced
1 tbsp golden syrup
1 tbsp water

YOU WILL NEED
12 squares of baking paper
    (8–10cm each)
2 oiled proving bags
large baking sheet lined with
    three layers of kitchen paper
cooking thermometer
large piping bag
small piping bag
1 chopstick

Orange and salted caramel doughnuts

If you think custard-filled doughnuts are good, you will love these. Tender and perfectly squishy, the orange-scented dough pillows are filled with the double delights of salted caramel sauce and caramel cream. With chocolate on top, they are sure to hit the spot.

1. Make the doughnut dough. Tip the flour, sugar, yeast and salt into the bowl of a stand mixer fitted with the dough hook. Make a well in the centre and add the milk, eggs, vanilla, butter and orange zest. Mix on medium–low speed for about 8 minutes, scraping down the inside of the bowl from time to time, until the dough is smooth and elastic, but still slightly sticky.

2. Shape the dough into a smooth ball and place it in a large, lightly oiled mixing bowl. Cover with a tea towel and leave to rise at room temperature for 1 hour, or overnight in the fridge, until doubled in size. (An overnight chill will make the dough easier to work with.)

3. Make the crème filling. While the dough is rising, tip 75g of the sugar into a small saucepan and add 1 tablespoon of water. Set the pan over a medium–low heat and, without stirring, dissolve the sugar. Bring the syrup to the boil and cook until it turns amber. Slide the pan off the heat and slowly and carefully add 100ml of the double cream.

4. Return the pan to a low heat to re-melt any hardened caramel. Add the butter and the sea-salt flakes, stir until smooth, pour into a bowl and leave to cool.

5. Using the same pan (no need to wash it), heat the milk with 35g of the remaining caster sugar and the vanilla pod until just below boiling.

6. Meanwhile, in a mixing bowl whisk together the egg yolks with the remaining 40g caster sugar and the cornflour for 1 minute, until smooth.

7. Pour the hot milk onto the egg yolks, whisking continuously until smooth. Return the mixture to the pan and cook, whisking continuously over a medium–low heat for about 1 minute, until the mixture thickens, just starts to bubble and you can no longer taste the cornflour. Strain the mixture into a clean bowl, add the orange zest, cover the surface of the custard with baking paper and leave to cool.

Continues overleaf

8. Shape the dough. Weigh the risen dough and divide it into 12 equal balls. Using your cupped hand, one by one, roll each dough ball against the work surface until smooth. Pinch the underside to neaten and place the ball on a square of baking paper.

9. Arrange the dough balls, on their squares, on two large baking sheets, slide the baking sheets each into an oiled proving bag and prove for 1–2 hours at room temperature, until light and puffy and doubled in size.

10. Cook the doughnuts. Pour the oil into a large, deep-sided frying pan (it shouldn't come more than halfway up the inside) or deep-fat fryer and place over a medium–high heat until it reads 170°C on a cooking thermometer. Tip the 250g caster sugar for coating into a tray.

11. Still on their paper squares, carefully drop 3–4 doughnuts at a time into the hot oil. Cook for 5 seconds, then remove the paper with tongs (it should slide from under each doughnut). Cook the doughnuts for about 1 minute, then turn them over and cook for another 1 minute. Then, turn again. Cook the doughnuts for about 4 minutes in total turning them every 45–60 seconds, until deep golden brown.

12. Using a slotted spoon, remove the doughnuts from the oil and drain them thoroughly on the kitchen-paper lined tray. Bring the oil back to temperature, and repeat to fry and drain the next batch of dough balls. Transfer the drained doughnuts to a wire rack and leave to cool.

13. Finish the crème. While the doughnuts are cooling, beat the cooled custard until smooth. In another bowl, whisk the remaining 100ml of cream to firm peaks. Fold the cream into the custard along with two thirds of the reserved caramel sauce, until combined. Scoop the crème into the large piping bag and the remaining caramel into the small piping bag. Set aside.

14. Make the chocolate glaze. Combine all the glaze ingredients with 1 tablespoon of water in a heatproof bowl and place it over a pan of barely simmering water. Stir to melt the chocolates. Remove from the heat and stir gently until smooth and glossy.

15. Assemble the doughnuts. Dip the underside of each cooled doughnut in the caster sugar. Using the chopstick, press a hole into the side of each doughnut and pipe a little caramel sauce into the middle of each, then pipe in the crème filling. Dip the top of the filled doughnuts in the chocolate glaze and leave to set for 15 minutes before serving.

Makes 4
Hands on 1 hour + resting and rising
Bake 40 mins

For the dough
110g active sourdough starter (see page 78)
1 tbsp olive oil, plus extra for greasing
500g strong white bread flour, plus 4 tbsp for dusting
12g ground sea-salt flakes
4–6 tbsp fine semolina

For the tomato sauce
1 tbsp olive oil
1 fat garlic clove, chopped
½ tsp crushed dried chillies
200g tinned chopped tomatoes
½ tsp caster sugar
salt and freshly ground black pepper

For the toppings
250g buffalo mozzarella bocconcini, drained and patted dry
100g 'nduja, torn into nuggets
12–16 slices spicy chilli and fennel seed salami
4 tbsp sliced roquito peppers or jalapeño chillies from a jar, drained and sliced
100g pitted black olives
4 tbsp freshly grated parmesan
small handful of basil or rocket
chilli oil, to serve

YOU WILL NEED
bench scraper
large baking tray, oiled
pizza stone or heavy baking sheet
pizza board or paddle (optional)

Calabrese sourdough pizza

These pizzas are hot and spicy – that is, they are warming as well as delicious (add more or less chilli to suit your taste, if you like), and perfect for sharing. Baking them on top of a pizza stone gives them a crisp crust. Make the dough the day before you plan to bake, and you'll need a sourdough starter – we've given you our recipe on the following page.

1. Make the dough. Mix the sourdough starter with 350ml of water in a large mixing bowl until combined. Add the olive oil and flour and mix with a rubber spatula to combine – there should be no dry flour in the bottom of the bowl, but the dough won't be smooth at this stage. Cover and set aside for 30 minutes at room temperature.

2. Add the ground sea salt to the dough with 1–2 tablespoons of water and, using one hand, mix to combine, twisting and squelching the dough between your fingers. Continue for about 1–2 minutes, until smooth and combined. Cover with a tea towel and leave for another 30 minutes.

3. You now need to stretch and fold the dough in the bowl four times – at 30-minute intervals over 2 hours. Using a wet hand, pick up the top edge of the dough, stretch it out slightly and fold it back over to meet the bottom edge. Turn the bowl 90° clockwise and repeat this stretching and folding a further 3 times, turning the bowl 90° after each fold. Cover and leave the dough to rest for 30 minutes.

4. Repeat the stretching and folding 3 more times, 30 minutes apart. The dough should feel silky smooth, aerated and very elastic. Cover the bowl with a tea towel and leave the dough to rise at room temperature for 2 hours, until bubbly and increased in size by about one-third.

5. Shape the dough. Turn out the dough onto a flightly floured work surface and divide it into 4 equal portions. Using a bench scraper and your hands, shape each portion into a tight ball. Place the balls, spaced well apart, on the oiled baking tray. Cover and chill overnight.

6. Make the tomato sauce. Heat the olive oil in a saucepan over a medium–low heat. Add the garlic and crushed chillies and cook for 1–2 minutes, until the garlic is soft but not coloured. Add the tomatoes, season with salt and pepper, then bring to the boil and cook for 5 minutes to thicken. Using a stick blender, blitz the sauce until smooth, adjust the seasoning and stir in the sugar to balance the acidity of the tomatoes. Leave to cool, then chill until you're ready to assemble the pizzas.

Continues overleaf

7. When you are ready to bake, heat the oven to 230°C/210°C fan/ Gas 8 or as hot as your oven will go, and place a pizza stone or baking sheet in the top third to heat up at the same time.

8. Assemble the pizzas. Combine the semolina with the extra 4 tablespoons of flour. Making one pizza at a time, dust a wooden board, pizza paddle or sheet of baking paper with some of the semolina mixture and place a dough portion in the middle. Using floured hands, gently pull and stretch the dough into a circle about 25cm in diameter, and with the edge thicker than the middle, to make a crust.

9. Spread 1 heaped tablespoon of the tomato sauce over the base, leaving a border, and tear one quarter of the mozzarella over the top. Scatter with a quarter of the 'nduja and the sliced salami, peppers or chillies and black olives. Sprinkle with a tablespoon of the parmesan and slide the pizza into the oven on top of the hot stone or baking sheet. Bake for 8–10 minutes, until the crust is golden brown and the top is bubbling. Serve immediately with torn basil or rocket leaves on top and a drizzle of chilli oil. Repeat to make 3 more pizzas.

Sourdough starter

You'll need 150g organic white bread flour and 150g organic rye or spelt flour, and lukewarm (never hot) water, as well as an airtight box.

Day 1 Combine the flours and store in an airtight box or jar. Mix 25g of the flour mixture with 25ml cool water in a glass or ceramic bowl and beat until smooth. Cover the bowl with baking paper, securing it with a rubber band, and leave it for 24 hours at room temperature. Total weight = 50g. **Day 2** Mix 25g of the flour mixture with 25ml lukewarm water to a paste and combine it with the Day 1 starter. Cover and set aside for 24 hours. Total weight = 100g. **Day 3** Discard half the mixture (50g). Add 25g of the flour mixture and 25ml lukewarm water to the remaining starter. Scoop into a glass jar. Cover loosely with the lid and set aside for 24 hours. Total weight = 100g. **Day 4** Repeat day 3. Total weight = 100g. **Day 5** Mix 100g of the flour mixture and 100ml lukewarm water to a paste and add this to the starter. Combine thoroughly, then cover loosely with the lid and leave for 24 hours. Total weight = 300g. **Day 6** Discard half the starter and add 75g of the flour mixture and 75ml water. Total weight = 300g. Your starter should be bubbly and have a fresh, yeasty smell. Repeat for another 6 days, keeping the ratio of flour to water the same at every feed.

Makes 6
Hands on 1 hour
+ rising and proving
Bake 15 mins

For the dough
300g strong white bread flour
30g light brown soft sugar
7g fast-action dried yeast
½ tsp salt
100ml whole milk, lukewarm
25g unsalted butter, softened
2 eggs, lightly beaten

For the raspberry jam
100g raspberries
100g jam sugar

For the icing
300g icing sugar, sifted

For the filling
400ml double cream
1 tsp vanilla paste

YOU WILL NEED
sugar thermometer
baking tray lined with
   baking paper
oiled proving bag
medium piping bag fitted
   with a medium open
   star nozzle
small piping bag

Fresh cream iced buns

I love these cakes. As a girl I would buy one every day from my local baker, on my way home from school – they remind me so much of my childhood.

1. Make the dough. Mix the flour, sugar, yeast and salt in a stand mixer fitted with a dough hook.

2. Pour the lukewarm milk into the mixer bowl. Add the butter and eggs and mix on low speed to combine. Scrape down the bowl, increase the speed slightly and knead for 6–8 minutes, until the dough is smooth and elastic. Turn the dough out of the bowl and shape it into a ball. Place the ball in a lightly oiled bowl, cover and leave to rise at room temperature for about 1 hour, or until doubled in size.

3. Make the jam. While the dough is rising, put the raspberries in a small saucepan, add the jam sugar and bring to the boil over a low heat. Crush the raspberries and sugar together with a potato masher, then when the sugar dissolves, increase the heat and boil for 4 minutes, until the temperature on a sugar thermometer reaches 105°C. Remove from the heat and pour the jam into a heatproof bowl. Leave to cool and set.

4. Shape the buns. Knock back the dough in the bowl, pressing it with your fingers to deflate, then turn it out onto a lightly floured work surface. Divide into 6 equal pieces, roll each into a neat ball, then into a tight sausage, about 10cm long, with the seam on the underside. Place the buns on the lined baking tray, leaving a 2cm gap between each. Slide the baking tray into an oiled proving bag and prove at room temperature for about 45 minutes, until puffy, doubled in size and joined together.

5. Heat the oven to 200°C/180°C fan/Gas 6.

6. Bake the buns. Bake for 12–15 minutes, until well risen and golden brown. Leave to cool completely on a wire rack.

7. Make the icing. While the buns are cooling, whisk the icing sugar in a wide, shallow bowl with about 3 tablespoons of cold water to make a smooth, thick paste. Once the buns are cold, dip the top of each one into the icing to coat, then return them to the wire rack to set.

8. Make the filling. Meanwhile, whip the cream with the vanilla until it forms soft peaks, then spoon it into the piping bag fitted with the medium open star nozzle. Once the icing has set, slice the buns horizontally, leaving one side still attached. Open up the buns and pipe the cream inside. Scoop the jam into the small piping bag, snip off the end, and pipe a wavy line of jam on top of the cream, ready to serve.

Makes 8
Hands on 15 mins
+ resting and rising
Cook about 20 mins

For the crumpets
125g plain flour
125g strong white bread flour
3.5g fast-action dried yeast
1 tsp caster sugar
1 tsp salt
250ml whole milk, lukewarm
½ tsp bicarbonate of soda
100ml lukewarm water
sunflower oil, for brushing

For the cheese sauce
25g unsalted butter
25g plain flour
200ml whole milk
125g mature cheddar, grated
1 tsp Dijon mustard
2 tsp Worcestershire sauce
1 egg yolk
salt and freshly ground
    black pepper

To serve
125g shredded ham hock
chilli sauce or pickles

YOU WILL NEED
flat griddle pan or heavy
    frying pan
8–9cm crumpet rings
    (preferably non-stick) x 4,
    lightly brushed with oil

Savoury crumpets

Toasted crumpets that catch pools of salty, melted butter are exactly what rainy weekends were made for... In this version, though, we're giving crumpets the toastie treatment and topping them with tangy cheese sauce and shredded ham hock – curl up on the sofa and enjoy.

1. Make the crumpets. Combine both the flours, with the yeast, sugar and salt in a mixing bowl and, using a balloon whisk, mix to evenly distribute the ingredients.

2. Add the warm milk and whisk for 1–2 minutes, until the batter is smooth. Cover the bowl and leave at room temperature for about 1 hour until the mixture has almost doubled in volume and the surface is covered in airy bubbles.

3. Add the bicarbonate of soda and warm water and whisk again until the mixture is smooth and thoroughly combined. Cover and leave at room temperature for 45 minutes, until the mixture is bubbly.

4. Place the griddle or frying pan over a medium–low heat and brush lightly with sunflower oil. Place the oiled crumpet rings on top. The pan is ready when it's hot enough to immediately sizzle a drop of water.

5. Ladle the crumpet mixture into the rings, filling each ring half to two-thirds full. Cook, over a medium–low heat, for about 8 minutes, until the top of the crumpets is dry and the surface is pocked with distinctive crumpet holes. Carefully remove the rings, turn the crumpets over and cook the other side for 1 minute, until golden.

6. Cool the cooked crumpets on a wire rack, brush the pan with oil again and re-oil the rings. Return them to the pan and cook the remaining mixture. Set aside to cool on a wire rack.

7. Make the cheese sauce. Melt the butter in a small saucepan over a medium heat. Add the flour and stir to combine, then cook for 30 seconds, stirring continuously, to form a paste.

8. Little by little, add the milk, stirring until the sauce is smooth. Once you've added all the milk, cook the sauce for another 1 minute, until it has thickened and the flour has been cooked out.

Continues overleaf

9. Slide the pan off the heat, add 100g of the grated cheese, and the Dijon mustard and Worcestershire sauce and season well with salt and pepper. Stir until the cheese has melted into the hot sauce. Add the egg yolk and mix again to combine.

10. Top and finish the crumpets. Preheat the grill to high and place the crumpets on a baking tray.

11. Divide two-thirds of the ham hock between the crumpets and spoon over the cheese sauce. Scatter the remaining grated cheese and ham hock over the top.

12. Grill the crumpets for about 1–2 minutes, until the sauce is bubbling and the cheese is golden brown. Serve with a splash of chilli sauce or a few pickles.

Makes 1
Hands on 40 mins + rising
Bake 25 mins

500g strong white bread flour
7g fast-action dried yeast
10g fine salt
1½ tbsp olive oil, plus extra
    for greasing
1 egg, lightly beaten with
    a pinch of salt

YOU WILL NEED
baking sheet dusted
    with flour
proving bag

Paul's seven-strand plaited wreath

This loaf is all about enjoying the process – kneading by hand and forming the plait, and then, of course, the satisfaction of the first, pillowy bite.

1. Make the dough. Place the flour in a large mixing bowl. Add the yeast to one side of the bowl and the salt to the other and stir to evenly mix.

2. Measure 340ml of water in a jug and pour three-quarters (225ml) of it into the flour mixture. Add the olive oil and mix by hand until combined, then mix in the rest of the water to form a dough. Turn out the dough onto a lightly floured work surface and knead by hand for about 10 minutes, until the dough looks silky and stretchy. Place the dough in a lightly oiled mixing bowl. Cover with a tea towel and leave to rise for about 45 minutes, until doubled in size.

3. Turn out the dough onto a lightly floured work surface again and knead it to knock it back. Shape the dough into a ball. Divide the ball into 7 equal pieces, then roll each piece into a strand about 50cm long.

4. Make the plait. Lay out the strands on a lightly floured work surface like an octopus, with the legs fanned out from a central, top point, stretching towards you. Stick all the ends at the central point to the work surface with your thumb. Take the outside strand on the right and cross it over 3 strands towards the middle, then take the outside strand on the left and cross it over 3 strands towards the middle.

5. Repeat this process, always taking the outside strand (first on the right and then on the left) and crossing it over 3 strands into the middle until you have plaited all of the strands.

6. Shape the plait. Trim each end of the plait to neaten, then form the plait into a wreath, pinching the ends together to join them and tucking the join underneath to give a neat finish. Place on the floured baking tray, then into a proving bag and leave the shaped loaf to prove for 45 minutes, until almost doubled in size.

7. Heat the oven to 220°C/200°C fan/Gas 8. Brush the top of the loaf with the beaten egg and bake for 25 minutes, until golden brown, and the loaf sounds hollow when tapped underneath.

Makes 12
Hands on 1 hour + rising and chilling
Bake 25 mins

For the dough
250g strong white bread flour
250g plain flour
50g caster sugar
7g fast-action dried yeast
½ tsp salt
200ml whole milk, lukewarm
2 eggs, lightly beaten
150g unsalted butter, softened

For the cinnamon filling
125g unsalted butter, softened
100g light brown soft sugar
1 tbsp tahini
4 tsp ground cinnamon
1 tsp cocoa powder
2 tbsp runny honey, to glaze

For the frosting
125g unsalted butter, softened
125g full-fat cream cheese,
   at room temperature
1 tsp vanilla paste
150g icing sugar

YOU WILL NEED
2 baking sheets, each lined
   with baking paper
33 x 23cm baking tin
   (6cm deep), lined
   (base and sides)
   with baking paper
proving bag

Iced cinnamon rolls

Whether you're looking for sweet solace over breakfast or a congratulatory treat at the end of a long day, these swirls are the answer. Make the dough the night before baking – it is much easier to handle when chilled.

1. Make the dough. Mix both flours with the caster sugar, yeast and salt in a stand mixer fitted with a dough hook. Add the lukewarm milk, and the eggs and butter and mix on low speed until combined. Increase the speed to medium and knead for 6–8 minutes to a smooth and elastic dough. Shape into a ball, return to the bowl, cover with a tea towel and chill for at least 4 hours, but ideally overnight, until doubled in size.

2. Make the filling. Beat the butter, brown sugar, tahini, cinnamon and cocoa in a bowl with a wooden spoon until smooth and creamy. Set aside.

3. Shape the buns. Turn out the dough onto a lightly dusted work surface, and cut it in half. Roll one piece into a neat 40 x 30cm rectangle, then halve it to make two 20 x 30cm rectangles. Using an offset palette knife, spread one-quarter of the cinnamon butter over one of the rectangles. Top with the second rectangle, then carefully transfer the 'sandwich' to a lined baking sheet and chill while you repeat with the other dough half.

4. Spread another quarter of the cinnamon butter over the top of the first dough sandwich, then carefully and neatly place the second dough sandwich on top. Cover and chill for 30 minutes.

5. Roll the dough stack on a lightly floured surface into a neat rectangle, about 48 x 25cm, with a long side nearest you. Spread the remaining cinnamon butter over the top. Starting with the side nearest to you, roll the dough into a neat, tight spiral. Using a sharp knife, trim the ends, then cut the roll into 12 equal slices. Place these cut-side up in the lined baking tin. Slide the tin into a proving bag, and prove at room temperature for about 45 minutes, until nearly doubled in size again.

6. Heat the oven to 180°C/160°C fan/Gas 4.

7. Bake the buns. Leaving them in the tin, bake the buns for 25 minutes, until well risen and golden brown. Remove from the oven and brush the tops with honey, then leave to cool for 10 minutes.

8. Make the frosting. Beat the butter until soft and pale. Add the cream cheese and vanilla, beat, then sift in the icing sugar and mix until smooth.

9. Decorate the buns. Spread half the frosting over the cooled buns, then leave to cool completely. Spread over the remaining frosting, to serve.

225ml whole milk
2 tsp lemon juice
450g '00' flour, plus
     extra for rolling out
1 tbsp baking powder
pinch of salt
75g caster sugar
125g unsalted butter,
     diced and chilled
75g sultanas
1 egg, beaten, to glaze

To serve
250g clotted cream
strawberry jam

YOU WILL NEED
6cm plain round cutter
baking sheet lined
     with baking paper

Fruit scones

Cream tea with lashings of clotted cream, spoonfuls of jam and towering scones – just warm from the oven, if you're really in need and can't wait. Using '00' (pasta) flour results in an especially soft and delicate crumb.

1. Heat the oven to 210°C/190°C fan/Gas 6–7.

2. Make the dough. Mix the milk and lemon juice in a jug and set it aside.

3. Sift the flour, baking powder and salt into a large mixing bowl. Add the sugar and mix to combine. Add the diced butter to the bowl and, using your fingertips, rub it into the dry ingredients until the mixture resembles breadcrumbs. Add the sultanas and mix to distribute evenly.

4. Make a well in the centre of the dry ingredients and add the milk and lemon mixture. With a round-bladed knife, mix the ingredients to combine, but do not overmix – the dough should hold together in a rough ball.

5. Shape the scones. Turn out the scone dough onto a lightly floured work surface and, using your hands, pat it into a rough 20 x 25cm rectangle. Fold the dough in half and pat it out again to 2.5cm thick.

6. Dip the cutter in flour and stamp out scones from the dough – be sure to firmly stamp in one push, rather than twisting (if you twist the cutter, you'll prevent the scones rising as they bake). Gently press the trimmings into a ball, flatten it out and stamp some more. You should get 10–12 scones altogether.

7. Bake the scones. Arrange the scones on the lined baking sheet, brush the tops with beaten egg and bake for about 17 minutes, until well risen and golden. Transfer to a wire rack to cool.

8. To serve, split each scone open and top each half with clotted cream and strawberry jam in whichever order you believe is right!

60g unsalted butter
200g drained sweetcorn
    kernels
½ tsp ground cumin
½ tsp smoked paprika
2 eggs
300ml buttermilk
175g plain flour
150g quick-cook polenta
2 tsp baking powder
1 tsp bicarbonate of soda
15g golden caster sugar
50g jalapeños, drained
    and chopped
5 spring onions, thinly sliced
100g smoked or mature
    cheddar, grated
2 tbsp finely chopped
    coriander
salt and freshly ground
    black pepper

YOU WILL NEED
ovenproof skillet or
    cast-iron pan (20cm
    diameter at the base)

Cornbread

A quick-and-easy, yeast-free bread, this cornbread is full of Southern States sunshine. It makes perfect company for a bowl of warming soup or chilli con carne – all in all a meal of genuine soul food. Use tinned sweetcorn for ease.

1. Melt the butter in the skillet or pan over a medium heat. Add the drained sweetcorn and cook, stirring often for about 5 minutes, until the kernels are starting to turn golden. Add the cumin and paprika and cook for a further 30 seconds. Tip the sweetcorn out of the pan into a bowl and leave to cool slightly. Do not wash the skillet.

2. Heat the oven to 200°C/180°C fan/Gas 6.

3. Whisk the eggs and buttermilk together in a jug.

4. Sift the flour, polenta, baking powder, bicarbonate of soda and sugar into a large mixing bowl. Season well with salt and black pepper and use a balloon whisk to combine.

5. Add the buttermilk mixture, buttery spiced sweetcorn, jalapeños, spring onions, cheese and coriander and mix to combine.

6. Scoop the mixture into the skillet, spread it level and bake the cornbread in the oven for 25 minutes, until it is risen and golden brown. Serve warm.

Pastry

Makes 6
Hands on 1 hour + chilling
Bake 45 mins

For the pastry
250g plain flour
250g strong white bread flour
100g lard, chilled and diced
100g unsalted butter,
    chilled and diced
150–175ml ice-cold water
1 tsp cider vinegar or white
    wine vinegar
salt and freshly ground
    black pepper
1–2 tbsp whole milk, to glaze

For the filling
350g lean beef steak (chuck,
    skirt or bavette are ideal),
    cut into 1–2cm pieces
250g (peeled weight) waxy
    potatoes (about 3 medium),
    cut into 1–2cm pieces
150g (peeled weight) swede,
    about ¼, cut into
    1–2cm pieces
1 large onion, finely chopped
1–2 tablespoons beef stock
60g salted butter or
    clotted cream

YOU WILL NEED
large baking tray, lined
    with baking paper

Cornish pasties

Wild coastlines, windswept beaches and sandy toes – eating hot, freshly baked Cornish pasties, wrapped in a paper bag, in the dunes is about as good as it gets. Ketchup and brown sauce are tasty on the side.

1. Make the pastry. Tip both flours into a large mixing bowl, add the lard and butter and season with salt and pepper. Using a table knife, cut the fats into the flour until the pieces are half their original size. Switch to using your fingertips to lightly rub the butter into the flour until there are only small pieces of fat visible, then make a well in the centre.

2. Add 150ml of the ice-cold water and add the vinegar, using the table knife until the pastry starts to clump together. Add a little more water if needed. Gather the dough into a ball and knead very gently for 10 seconds until smooth. Flatten the dough into a disc, wrap and chill for 1 hour, until firm.

3. Make the filling. While the pastry is chilling, tip the beef, potatoes, swede and onion into a bowl. Add the beef stock and season generously with salt and pepper and mix well to combine.

4. Assemble the pasties. Lightly dust the work surface with flour, and divide the pastry into 6 equal portions. Roll out each portion until about 3mm thick and, using a side plate or cake tin as a guide, cut the pastry into six 20cm-diameter discs.

5. Lay the pastry discs on the work surface, divide the filling between each one, mounding it evenly in the middle of the pastry and top with a nugget of butter or spoonful of clotted cream.

6. Brush one side of each pastry disc with water and fold the other side over to make a half-moon shape, then press the edges together to seal. Crimp the edges, arrange them on a lined baking tray and chill the pasties for 30 minutes, or until ready to bake.

7. Heat the oven to 190°C/170°C fan/Gas 5.

8. Bake the pasties. Brush the top of each pasty with milk. Cut a small hole in the top and bake for 40–45 minutes, until the pastry is crisp and golden, and the filling is steaming hot and cooked through.

Serves 10
Hands on 1½ hours
Bake 45 mins

For the pastry
300g strong white bread
    flour, plus extra if needed
¼ tsp fine salt
140ml lukewarm water
1½ tbsp olive oil
cornflour, for dusting
100g butter, melted
1 large egg yolk
1 tbsp sesame seeds
1 tbsp crushed sea salt

For the filling
1 tbsp olive oil
1 large onion, chopped
2 garlic cloves, crushed
900g baby leaf spinach
finely grated zest of 1 lemon
25g flat-leaf parsley, leaves
    picked and tender stems
    finely chopped
25g dill, leaves and stems
    finely chopped
⅛ tsp freshly grated nutmeg
1 large egg, beaten
200g feta cheese, crumbled
salt and freshly ground
    black pepper

For the tzatziki
¼ cucumber
¼ tsp salt
150g full-fat Greek yoghurt
1 small garlic clove,
    crushed or finely grated
1 tbsp extra-virgin olive oil
1 tsp white wine vinegar
1 tsp tzatziki seasoning

Continues overleaf

Paul's Spanakopita

Conjuring up the chilled vibes of a beachside Greek taverna, spanakopita evokes all the delicious contentment of any favourite holiday. The crisp filo pastry is homemade in this recipe, and rolled out using a pasta machine to save time. But, of course, if you don't fancy the challenge of homemade filo, shop-bought will do the job (Paul says so).

1. Make the pastry dough. Sift the flour and salt into a bowl and make a well in the middle. Mix the water and oil together and gradually pour it onto the flour, mixing as you go. You're looking for a soft, but not sticky dough. If the mixture is too wet, add a sprinkling more of flour.

2. Once the dough has come together, take it out of the bowl and start kneading. It should be at a consistency where you shouldn't need any flour to knead it. Work the dough for about 10 minutes, or until it looks smooth. Place it in an airtight container and rest it in the fridge for 1 hour.

3. Make the filling. While the dough is resting, heat the oil in a large, wide pan over a medium heat. Add the onion and fry for 5–7 minutes, until soft. Remove the pan from the heat and stir in the garlic, then scrape the onions and garlic into a large mixing bowl and leave to cool.

4. Return the pan to a medium heat. Add the spinach, squashing it down if necessary. Season with salt and pepper and put the lid on the pan. Leave the spinach to wilt for about 5 minutes, removing the lid to stir occasionally, until it's completely cooked. Drain it into a colander and press it with the back of a spoon to get rid of as much liquid as possible. Press with kitchen paper to remove any excess moisture.

5. Add the spinach to the bowl with the onion and garlic and leave to cool. Once cooled, add the lemon zest, parsley, dill and nutmeg, and season with salt and pepper. Stir in the beaten egg, then fold in the crumbled feta. Set aside.

6. Lay out the sheet of baking paper on your work surface and dust it generously with cornflour. Heat the oven to 200°C/180°C fan/Gas 6.

7. Make the pastry sheets. Divide the rested dough into 5 equal balls.

8. One ball at a time, flatten each dough portion to a rough rectangle using a rolling pin. Sprinkle your hands and the pastry rectangle liberally

Continues overleaf

Paul's Spanakopita (continued)

YOU WILL NEED
90cm sheet of non-stick
   baking paper
pasta machine
26cm springform tin,
   greased with melted butter,
   base and ring separated

with cornflour. Pass the portion through the pasta machine, working from the widest setting to the thinnest setting, until you have a thin length of pastry about 70cm long. Using the backs of your hands gently stretch the pastry sheet widthways until you can almost see through it. Don't worry about the odd hole, as the layers should cover this up. You should have a long, rectangular sheet measuring about 90 x 17cm. Lay the pastry onto the cornflour-dusted baking paper and brush with melted butter.

9. Repeat for each of the remaining balls of dough. Each time you roll a sheet of pastry, lay it over the top of the previous sheet, brushing with butter between each layer. Continue until you have finished the pastry.

10. Place the spinach filling along one of the long edges of the rectangle. Fold over the short ends of the pastry (this prevents any filling escaping as you roll it up). Using the baking paper underneath to help, roll up the spinach inside the pastry, so that you form a long sausage shape. Then, starting at one end, curve the sausage into a spiral shape and gently slide it onto the buttered base of the springform tin.

11. Add the egg yolk to the remaining melted butter and brush this over the top and sides of the spanakopita. Sprinkle with the sesame seeds and crushed sea salt and secure the buttered tin ring to the base. Bake the spanakopita for 40–45 minutes, until the pastry is dark golden-brown and the filling is piping hot.

12. Make the tzatziki. While the spanakopita is baking, grate the cucumber into a sieve set over a bowl and sprinkle over the salt. Mix the salt into the cucumber in the sieve, then leave to drain for 10 minutes. Squeeze any remaining liquid out of the cucumber with your hands.

13. Spoon the yoghurt into a bowl, add the drained cucumber, along with the garlic, olive oil, white wine vinegar and tzatziki seasoning and fold together. Transfer to a serving bowl and chill until required.

14. Once the spanakopita is ready, remove it from the oven. Serve warm or cold in slices with the tzatziki in a bowl on the side.

Makes 8
Hands on 2 hours
+ marinating and chilling
Bake 60 mins

1kg skinless, boneless chicken
   thigh fillets, cut into
   bite-sized pieces

For the marinade
4 fat garlic cloves, crushed
thumb-sized piece of ginger,
   peeled and finely grated
1 green chilli, finely chopped
   with seeds
juice of 1 lime
2 tsp garam masala
1 tsp ground cumin
1 tsp turmeric powder
1 tsp chilli powder
200g full-fat natural yoghurt
salt and freshly ground
   black pepper

For the sauce
2 onions, chopped
1 tbsp ghee or butter
3 fat garlic cloves, crushed
thumb-sized piece of ginger,
   finely grated
1 green chilli, finely chopped
   (deseed if you want
   less heat)
2 tsp ground cumin
2 tsp chilli powder
2 tsp garam masala
1 tsp ground fenugreek
2 bay leaves
2 tbsp tomato purée
1 x 400g tin of chopped
   tomatoes
1 tbsp light brown soft sugar
200g tinned green lentils,
   drained
75ml double cream
25g unsalted butter
25g ground almonds
3 tbsp finely chopped
   coriander

Continues overleaf

Friday night curry pies

*Friday night, pie night; or Friday night, curry night... whatever your
tradition, these have it covered. Bake as many as you need, depending on
who's in for supper, and freeze the remainder for an easy win next week.
Serve with a selection of Indian pickles and perhaps some sag aloo.*

1. Marinate the chicken. Mix all the marinade ingredients together in
a large mixing bowl. Season with salt and pepper, then add the chicken
and mix well until coated. Cover and leave the chicken to marinate
in the fridge for at least 4 hours, but preferably overnight.

2. Make the sauce. The next day, tip the onions into a large pan, add the
ghee or butter and cook over a medium–low heat for about 8 minutes,
stirring often, until softened. Add the garlic, ginger and chilli and cook
for a further 1 minute.

3. Increase the heat slightly and add the spices to the pan, mix to
combine and cook for about 2 minutes, until the mixture is aromatic.
Add the bay leaves and tomato purée and cook for another 1 minute,
stirring continuously, before adding the chopped tomatoes and sugar.
Fill the tomato tin to the top with water (400ml) and add that too.
Season well with salt and pepper and bring to the boil. Reduce the heat
to low, cover and simmer, stirring occasionally, for about 45 minutes,
until the sauce is rich and slightly thickened.

4. Meanwhile, heat the oven 220°C/200°C fan/Gas 7.

5. Line a baking tray or shallow roasting tin with foil and arrange the
marinated chicken pieces on top in a single layer. Bake in the oven for
about 20 minutes, until cooked through and starting to char at the edges.

6. When the sauce is ready, blend with a stick blender until smooth.
Add the lentils, cream, butter and ground almonds, mix to combine and
adjust the seasoning to taste. Add the cooked chicken pieces and the
coriander, stir to combine and leave to cool.

7. Make the pastry. While the sauce is cooling, tip the flour into a large
mixing bowl, season with salt and pepper and add the chilled, diced
butter. Using a table knife, cut the butter into the flour until the pieces
are half their original size. Switch to using your fingertips to lightly
rub the butter into the flour until there are only small pieces of butter
visible, then make a well in the centre of the mixture.

Continues overleaf

Friday night curry pies (continued)

For the pastry
600g plain flour
350g unsalted butter,
    chilled and diced
8 tbsp ice-cold water
1 tbsp cider vinegar or
    white wine vinegar
1 egg, lightly beaten,
    for glazing
1 tbsp black onion seeds

YOU WILL NEED
13cm round foil pie dishes
    x 8 (about 3–4cm deep)

8. Mix in the ice-cold water and vinegar with the table knife until the pastry starts to clump together. Gather the dough into a ball and knead gently for 20 seconds, until smooth. Flatten the dough into a disc, place it in an airtight container and chill it for 2 hours, until firm.

9. Assemble the pies. Lightly dust the work surface with flour and divide the pastry into 8 equal portions. Take a portion of pastry and cut it into 2 unequal pieces – one twice as large as the other. Roll out the larger piece into a neat disc, about 20cm in diameter and 2–3mm thick. Use the pastry disc to line a foil pie dish, pressing it evenly into the base and up the sides, leaving a slight overhang. Repeat with the remaining pastry and pie dishes, making 8 pie cases in total.

10. Divide the cooled pie filling between the cases. Roll the smaller pieces of pastry into neat 15cm discs, large enough to generously cover the top of the pies. Brush the edge of each pie with water and lay a pastry disc on top to cover the filling. Pinch the edges to seal and trim off any excess pastry. Cover and chill for 20 minutes.

11. Meanwhile, heat the oven to 190°C/170°C fan/Gas 5 and place 2 baking sheets in the oven to heat up at the same time.

12. Bake the pies. Brush the top of each pie with the beaten egg and sprinkle with the onion seeds. Cut a small hole in each pie lid and bake for 35–40 minutes, until the filling is piping hot and the pastry golden brown and crisp.

Serves 8–10
Hands on 2 hours + chilling
Bake 1¾ hours

For the pastry
400g plain flour
200g caster sugar
2 tsp baking powder
pinch of salt
200g unsalted butter,
    at room temperature, diced
1 large egg, lightly beaten
1 tsp vanilla extract

For the almond paste
150g ground almonds
150g caster sugar
finely grated zest of
    ¼ unwaxed lemon
1 egg, beaten

For the filling
1.5kg apples, such as
    Bramley or Cox, peeled,
    cored and cut into
    thin slices
60g caster sugar
3 tsp ground cinnamon
2 tbsp lemon juice,
    about ½ lemon

YOU WILL NEED
23cm, deep springform
    tin, greased
baking beans or rice
baking tray

Dutch apple pie

*This is my mum's apple pie – she would always make it for birthdays
and other celebrations, so, to me, it truly represents the comfort of home.
I bake it whenever I am homesick or I just want to feel closer to my family.
Almond paste is used in a lot of Dutch bakes and, in this recipe, it keeps
the bottom of the pie from becoming soggy, and also makes it extra tasty.
You can freeze any leftover and use it another time.*

1. Make the pastry. Add the flour, sugar, baking powder and salt to a large
mixing bowl. Rub in the butter using your fingertips until the mixture
forms breadcrumbs. Mix in the egg and vanilla with a table knife, then
with your hands until it comes together into a ball, but do not overwork
it. Divide the pastry in 2 unequal pieces of two-thirds and one-third.
Flatten each piece into a disc, wrap and chill for 1 hour, until firm.

2. Make the almond paste. While the pastry is chilling, combine the
ground almonds, sugar and lemon zest in a large bowl and knead in
half the beaten egg to make a pliable paste, adding a little more egg
if needed. Cover and chill for at least 1 hour (you can make the paste
the night before, if you prefer). Reserve the remaining egg to glaze.

3. Make the pastry case. Roll out the larger portion of pastry on
a lightly floured work surface into a 35cm-diameter circle, about 3mm
thick. Line the cake tin with the pastry, pressing it neatly and evenly
over the base and up the sides. Using a sharp knife, trim the excess
from the top and chill the pastry case for 20 minutes.

4. Heat the oven to 180°C/160°C fan/Gas 4.

5. Line the pastry-lined tin with baking paper and fill it with baking
beans or rice. Bake for 20 minutes, until the edges of the pastry
are crisp and start to turn golden.

6. Make the filling and lattice topping. While the pastry case is baking,
mix the apples with the sugar, cinnamon and lemon juice in a large bowl.
Set aside.

7. Remove the paper and beans or rice and bake the pastry case for
a further 5 minutes to cook the base. Leave to cool slightly.

8. Lightly dust the work surface with flour and roll out the remaining
pastry into a neat 25cm-diameter circle, about 3–4mm thick. Cut the

Continues overleaf

pastry into sixteen 1cm-wide strips for the lattice top. Arrange the strips on a baking tray and return them to the fridge for 10 minutes to firm up slightly to make them easier to handle.

9. Roll out the chilled almond paste into a 21cm-diameter round and place it in the bottom of the cooked pastry case. Fill the pastry case with the apple mixture, either neatly arranging them so that the apples lie flat, or just tip the whole bowl in and pat the slices flat with your fingers.

10. Lattice the strips of pastry over the apple filling, interweaving them under and over each other, until the top is covered (see page 126 for a step-by-step method, if necessary). Trim the excess pastry and crimp the edges to seal. Brush with the reserved beaten egg.

11. Bake the pie. Put the tin in the oven and bake for 1–1¼ hours, until the top is golden brown and the apples are tender. If you think the pastry is browning too quickly, cover the top loosely with foil. Leave to cool for 10 minutes before removing the pie from the tin. Serve warm or at room temperature.

Variations

You can add 75g of raisins, currants or other dried fruit to the filling to give the recipe your own twist. Make sure to soak the dried fruit for at least 15 minutes in lukewarm water and pat dry before adding it to the apple filling. Another option is to add 150g of chopped nuts of your choice to the filling. Instead of doing pastry lattice work, you could make decorations out of the leftover dough, such as flowers or leaves, to place on top of the pie.

Serves 6
Hands on 1 hour + chilling
Bake 55 mins

For the pastry
250g unsalted butter, chilled
150g plain flour
100g strong white bread flour
pinch of salt
100–125ml ice-cold water
1 tsp lemon juice or
    white wine vinegar
1 egg, lightly beaten, to glaze

For the topping
2 red peppers,
    halved and deseeded
1 tbsp olive oil
250g ricotta cheese
2 garlic cloves, crushed
2 tbsp finely grated
    parmesan cheese
2 thyme sprigs, leaves picked
finely grated zest of
    ½ unwaxed lemon
2 courgettes, cut into
    long, thin strips with
    a vegetable peeler
1 bunch of asparagus,
    trimmed and cut into
    long diagonal slices
100g feta cheese
25g pine nuts
1 handful of basil leaves
    or rocket
2 tbsp extra-virgin olive oil
salt and freshly ground
    black pepper

YOU WILL NEED
2 large baking sheets,
    1 lined with baking paper

Med veg puff tart

Homemade puff pastry is worth every moment of quiet kitchen time.
And because the buttery, flaky pastry is where all that meditative effort lies,
here it is simply topped with colourful veggies and three different cheeses.

1. Make the pastry. (This takes at least 2–3 hours; it is best made
the day before to allow plenty of resting time.) Dice 50g of the chilled
butter. Combine both flours in a mixing bowl, add the salt and the
diced butter and rub them in using your fingertips until the mixture
resembles fine breadcrumbs.

2. Make a well in the centre of the dry ingredients, add 100ml of the
ice-cold water and the lemon juice or vinegar and combine using a table
knife. Bring the dough together, adding up to 25ml more water if needed,
but do not allow the dough to become too wet. Bring it into a ball, flatten
into a neat rectangle, place in an airtight container and chill for 1 hour.

3. Roll out the dough on a lightly floured work surface to a rectangle
measuring 45 x 15cm (it must be three times as long as it is wide) with
one of the short ends nearest to you.

4. Place the remaining 200g of butter between 2 sheets of baking paper
and use a rolling pin to flatten it into a neat square that is slightly smaller
than one third of the pastry rectangle, about 13cm square. Place the
butter on the middle third of the pastry rectangle and fold the bottom
third up over it, brush off any excess flour and fold the top third down
so that the butter is completely encased.

5. Turn the square 90° clockwise and lightly dust the work surface and
rolling pin with flour. Roll out the pastry again into a neat straight-sided
rectangle of a similar size as before. Use short, sharp tapping and rolling
actions rather than long sweeping rolls and use your hands to try to keep
the pastry as neat as possible as you roll it out. Fold the dough the same
way as before: the bottom third of the rectangle goes up over the middle
third and the top third comes down, brushing off any excess flour each
time. Turn the square 90° clockwise, place it in an airtight container and,
keeping the square flat and in the same rotation, chill for 45 minutes.

6. Lightly dust the work surface with flour and roll out the dough again
into the same size rectangle, keeping the sides and ends as neat as
possible. Fold the dough up as before, turn the square 90° clockwise

Continues overleaf

and repeat this roll and fold. Pace in an airtight container, keeping the square in the same position, and chill again for 45 minutes.

7. Repeat this rolling and folding once more to make a total of 4 rolls and folds. Cover and chill the pastry for at least 2 hours before using.

8. Heat the oven to 200°C/180°C fan/Gas 6.

9. Prepare the toppings. Place the peppers skin-side up on a baking tray. Drizzle with the olive oil and roast for about 20 minutes, until the skin starts to blacken and blister. Leave the peppers to cool, then peel off the skin and cut the flesh into 2cm-wide strips.

10. Mix the ricotta with the garlic, parmesan, thyme leaves and lemon zest. Season well with salt and pepper. Set aside.

11. Blind bake the base. Roll out the pastry on a lightly floured work surface to a neat rectangle of 40 x 30cm, and trim the sides to neaten. Place the pastry on the lined baking sheet and score a 2–3cm-wide border around the edge with a sharp knife. Prick the base with a fork and chill for 30 minutes. Meanwhile, place the second baking sheet in the oven to heat up.

12. Brush the border of the pastry with beaten egg and slide the baking sheet onto the one already in the oven. Bake the pastry for 20 minutes, until the border is golden and the base has puffed up.

13. Assemble and finish the tart. Spread the ricotta mixture evenly over the middle of the pastry, within the border, then arrange the peppers, courgette strips and asparagus on top. Crumble the feta over the vegetables and scatter with the pine nuts. Season with salt and pepper and bake for a further 25–30 minutes, until the pastry is crisp and the toppings start to brown at the edges.

14. Leave the tart to cool for 10 minutes, then serve warm or at room temperature scattered with basil or rocket and with a drizzle of extra-virgin olive oil to finish.

Makes 12
Hands on 1½ hours
+ chilling and setting
Bake 35 mins

For the pastry
200g plain flour
20g ground almonds
40g icing sugar, sifted
pinch of salt
125g unsalted butter,
    chilled and diced
1 egg yolk
1 tsp vanilla extract
2 tsp ice-cold water

For the jam
100g raspberries
100g jam sugar
juice of ½ lemon

For the frangipane
75g unsalted butter, softened
75g caster sugar
75g ground almonds
1 egg, lightly beaten
1 tsp almond extract
finely grated zest of
    ½ unwaxed lemon

To decorate
250g icing sugar, sifted
½ tsp almond extract
drop of red food colouring
6 glacé cherries, halved

YOU WILL NEED
sugar thermometer
6cm round tart rings x 12
baking sheet lined with
    baking paper
10–12cm squares of
    baking paper x 12,
    scrunched to soften
baking beans or rice
large piping bag
small piping bag

Cherry Bakewell tarts

For me, cherry Bakewell tarts are the ultimate comfort food. I vividly remember having a brew and Bakewell tart with my nan in front of the television – among my happiest memories. I hope you enjoy these as much as I do!

1. Make the pastry. Mix the flour, ground almonds, icing sugar and salt in a food processor or a mixing bowl until combined. Rub in the butter with your fingertips or pulse in the processor, until the mixture resembles breadcrumbs.

2. In a small bowl, use a fork to lightly whisk the egg yolk with the vanilla and ice-cold water until combined. Pour the egg mixture into the dry ingredients in the bowl or processor and mix or pulse until the pastry clumps together into a dough.

3. Tip out the dough onto a lightly floured work surface and gently knead it into a neat ball. Flatten the dough into a disc, cover and chill in the fridge for 1 hour.

4. Make the jam. While the dough is chilling, put the raspberries in a small saucepan. Add the jam sugar and lemon juice and slowly bring the mixture to the boil over a low heat. Crush the raspberries and sugar together with a potato masher, then when the sugar dissolves, increase the heat and boil for a further 4 minutes, until the temperature on a sugar thermometer reaches 105°C. Remove from the heat and carefully pour the jam into a heatproof bowl. Leave to cool and set.

5. Make the pastry cases. Roll out the pastry on a lightly floured work surface until about 2mm thick. Using the tart rings, stamp out 12 rounds of pastry, then lift the pastry, still inside the ring, onto the lined baking sheet.

6. Re-roll any pastry trimmings into a rectangle about 30 x 19cm. Cut the rectangle into 12 strips, about 2.5cm wide (slightly wider than the depth of the tart rings) and 19cm long. Line the inside of the tart rings with the pastry strips and use your fingers to gently press the base and sides together where they join. Prick the base of each pastry case and chill the pastry cases in the fridge for 20 minutes.

7. Heat the oven to 180°C/160°C fan/Gas 4.

Continues overleaf

8. Using a sharp knife, carefully trim the edge of each pastry case to align with the top of the tart ring. Line each tart with a scrunched square of baking paper and fill with baking beans or rice.

9. Put the baking sheet with the tart rings in the oven and bake the cases for 10 minutes, until the edge of each case starts to turn crisp and golden. Remove the paper and beans or rice and bake for a further 8–10 minutes, until golden.

10. Make the frangipane. Meanwhile, use an electric hand whisk to beat the butter and caster sugar together until pale and creamy. Add the remaining frangipane ingredients and mix together until combined. Scoop the mixture into the large piping bag, and snip the end to make a 1cm opening.

11. Assemble and bake the tarts. Spread a scant teaspoon of jam into the base of each cooked pastry case. Pipe the frangipane into the tarts, filling each one three-quarters full, then bake them for about 15 minutes, until the frangipane is golden and springs back when pressed in the centre. Leave to cool completely on the baking sheet, then remove the tarts from the rings.

12. Decorate the tarts. Mix the icing sugar with 2 tablespoons of water and the almond extract to a thick but spreadable consistency. Scoop 1 tablespoon of the icing into a separate bowl and add a drop of red food colouring, then mix to combine and scoop the coloured icing into the small piping bag.

13. Cover each tart with the white icing, spreading it out evenly. Cut a small hole in the piping bag and pipe thin and even horizontal red lines across the white icing. While the icing is still wet, take a cocktail stick and lightly drag it through the icing first in one direction, then in the other to give a feather effect. Finally, top each tart with a glacé cherry half and leave the icing to set before serving.

Makes 12
Hands on 2 hours + resting, chilling and proving
Bake 15 mins

___

For the dough
500g strong white flour
25g caster sugar
7g fast-action dried yeast
1 tsp salt
150ml whole milk
275g unsalted butter
1 egg, lightly beaten, to glaze

For the filling
175g ground almonds
150g icing sugar
15g unsalted butter,
   at room temperature
finely grated zest of ¼ lemon
1 tsp almond extract
1 egg white
pinch of salt

To decorate
50g flaked almonds
100g icing sugar, sifted
juice of ½ lemon

YOU WILL NEED
20 x 25cm tray or plastic
   box, lightly oiled
2 baking sheets, each lined
   with baking paper
2 proving bags

Almond bear claws

These pastries are brilliant fun to make with budding bakers (and for you to enjoy with a mug of coffee at the end). For the best results, begin the pastry the day before you want to eat them. Don't be put off by the long method – most of that is resting and chilling, making the hands-on work not too arduous at all and a lovely way to pass the time on a free weekend together.

1. Make the dough. Combine the flour, sugar, yeast and salt in the bowl of a stand mixer fitted with a dough hook.

2. Heat the milk with 160ml of water until lukewarm. Add 25g of the butter and leave it for 30 seconds to soften and start to melt. Pour the warm milk mixture into the bowl and mix on medium–low speed to combine. Scrape down the inside of the bowl and continue to mix for about 3 minutes, until the dough is nearly smooth – it should not be elastic at this stage, but the ingredients thoroughly combined.

3. Turn out the dough and shape it into a 20cm square on a lightly floured work surface. Place the square in the lightly oiled tray or plastic box, cover and chill for 2–4 hours, or ideally overnight.

4. Just before the dough is ready, cut the remaining butter into quarters and lay the butter slices side by side on a sheet of baking paper. Cover with more paper. Use a rolling pin to press and roll the butter into a neat 16cm square. Leave the butter square covered and chill it for 30 minutes.

5. Roll out the dough on a lightly floured work surface to a neat 50 x 18cm rectangle. With a long side nearest you, place the chilled butter in the middle of the dough and fold the left side of the dough over the butter to cover, brush off any excess flour and fold the right side over the top. Lightly press the open sides together to seal in the butter.

6. Turn the dough through 90°, flour the work surface and, starting at the middle of the dough and using a short, sharp tapping action with the rolling pin, flatten and then gently roll the dough into a neat 50 x 18cm rectangle again, keeping the sides and ends neat and straight.

7. With a short side nearest you, fold the top edge of the dough down to the middle and the bottom edge up to meet it. Gently press together, brush off any excess flour and then fold the dough in half again so that you have a dough package that is now 4 layers thick. Turn the dough 90° clockwise so that the opening is on the right, then cover and chill it for 30–45 minutes to relax the gluten and firm up the butter.

Continues overleaf

8. Prepare the almond filling. While the dough is chilling, combine all the filling ingredients in the bowl of a stand mixer fitter with the beater. Weigh the mixture and divide it into 6 equal portions. Roll each portion into a long, thin 24cm sausage. Wrap the rolls tightly in baking paper and chill until you're ready to use them.

9. Finish the dough. Roll out the dough on a lightly floured work surface to a neat rectangle. With a short side nearest to you, fold the top third down to the middle, brush off any excess flour and fold the bottom third up to cover it. Wrap and chill for a further 1 hour.

10. Assemble the pastries. Cut the dough in half, cover and return one half to the fridge. Roll out the remaining half on a lightly floured work surface to a 26 x 38cm rectangle with a long side nearest to you. Trim the ends to neaten. Cut the dough vertically into three equal-sized 12 x 24cm rectangles.

11. Place one of the almond-paste rolls vertically 2cm in from the left edge of the first dough piece. Brush the dough to the right of the almond roll with beaten egg and fold the dough over the roll to cover, pressing to seal in the filling. Brush the other side of the dough with egg and fold this over to create a flap, pressing to seal the seam.

12. Turn the roll over so that the seam is on the underside. Cut the roll in half and cut six 1cm-deep slashes into the flap of each pastry. Gently bend the pastry to form a C-shape and to open up the 'claws'. Place on the lined baking sheet.

13. Repeat steps 11 and 12 to make a further 4 pastries from this portion of dough. Slide the baking sheet into a proving bag and repeat with the second dough portion and almond paste, making 12 pastries in total. Leave to prove on the lined baking sheets at room temperature for about 1 hour, until the dough is puffy and risen by about half again.

14. Heat the oven to 190°C/170°C fan/Gas 5.

15. Bake the pastries. Brush the pastries with beaten egg, scatter with flaked almonds and bake for about 15 minutes, until crisp and golden brown. Leave to cool on the trays.

16. Make the icing and decorate. Whisk the icing sugar with the lemon juice until smooth and the icing will just hold a ribbon trail when you lift the whisk. (Add a little water if needed, to make the icing the right consistency.) Using a teaspoon, drizzle the icing over each pastry and leave to set before serving.

Serves 6
Hands on 30 mins + chilling
Bake 40 mins

For the pastry
450g plain flour
pinch of salt
100g margarine or unsalted
    butter, cubed and chilled
100g lard, cubed and chilled
6 tbsp ice-cold water

For the filling
1 large white onion,
    chopped into 1cm dice
300g mature cheddar,
    coarsely grated
1 egg, lightly beaten with
    a pinch of salt, to glaze

YOU WILL NEED
20cm pie dish (4cm deep),
    greased

Mum's cheese and onion pie

A traditional Northern delicacy, this pie has been a family favourite for as long as I can remember – it was a regular in my mum's rotation of weekday teatimes, and mostly served with baked beans and chips. It became part of my repertoire at university, and now my husband is an avid fan, too. For me, then, it is the ultimate comfort food, filled with lots of great memories that make me smile. I use lard in my pastry, for its flakiness, but you could use all margarine or butter for a veggie option. And mixing and matching the cheeses with your favourites is also fun. Then, you could add more heat with a teaspoon of cayenne pepper or mustard powder sprinkled in. And a recent revelation from my sister is the addition of chopped chorizo. Enjoy!

1. Make the pastry. Mix the flour and salt in a large mixing bowl. Rub in the margarine or butter and lard with your fingertips to a breadcrumb consistency. Using a table knife, mix in enough of the cold water to bring the dough together. Gather the dough with your hands and shape it into a ball. Divide the pastry into 2 unequal pieces of two-thirds and one-third. Flatten each piece into a disc, cover and chill for about 1 hour.

2. Start the filling. While the pastry is chilling, tip the onion into a pan. Add a splash of water and set the pan over a medium–low heat. Steam-cook the onion, stirring occasionally, for 5 minutes, until soft and the water evaporates. Leave to cool.

3. Heat the oven to 200°C/180°C fan/Gas 6.

4. Assemble the pie. Roll out the larger piece of pastry on a lightly floured work surface, until about 3–4mm thick. Use the disc to line the pie dish, pressing it into the base and up the sides and trimming any excess. Scatter half of the cheddar into the pastry case, top with the cooled onion, then add the remaining cheese.

5. Roll out the remaining pastry into a disc, about 28cm in diameter, to make the pie lid.

6. Brush the beaten egg around the edge of the filled pastry case and top with the lid, pressing the edges together to seal. Using a sharp knife, trim off any excess pastry and crimp the edges – you can do this by pressing down the edge with the back of a fork, if you are not an expert crimper.

7. Brush more beaten egg over the pie and cut 3 slits in the top with a knife. Bake the pie for about 40 minutes, until the pastry is crisp and golden brown.

Makes 24
Hands on 1¼ hours
+ chilling and resting
Bake 20 mins

For the puff pastry
300g unsalted butter, chilled
175g plain flour
125g strong white bread flour
1 tsp salt
125–150ml ice-cold water
2 tsp lemon juice

For the filling
2 rosemary sprigs, leaves
    picked and finely chopped
2 fat garlic cloves, crushed
4 tbsp fig conserve or chutney
8 slices of prosciutto
200g taleggio, rind removed,
    and cut into 5mm–1cm dice
4 tbsp finely grated parmesan
1 egg, beaten
freshly ground black pepper

YOU WILL NEED
pizza wheel (optional)
2 large baking sheets, each
    lined with baking paper

Prosciutto, taleggio and fig twists

*These cheese straws are so perfect you'll want to reserve them for nights
in with your most favourite friends: tangy taleggio, silky prosciutto and
a sophisticated sweep of fig relish all wrapped into buttery, flaky pastry.*

1. Make the pastry. Dice 50g of the chilled butter and tip it into a mixing
bowl. Add both flours and the salt and rub in the butter using your hands.
Make a well in the centre, add 125ml of the ice-cold water, and the lemon
juice, and mix with a table knife to bring the dough together. Add up to
25ml more water, if needed. Gather the dough into a ball, flatten it into
a neat square, place in an airtight container and chill for 1 hour.

2. Roll out the dough on a lightly floured work surface to a 15 x 45cm
rectangle (three times as long as it is wide). Turn it, if necessary, so that
one of the short ends is nearest to you. Cut the remaining 250g of cold
butter into 2cm slices and place these between 2 sheets of baking paper.
Using a rolling pin, flatten the butter into a neat 14cm square.

3. Place the butter onto the middle section of the pastry and fold the
bottom third up over it, brush off any excess flour and fold the top third
down so that the butter is completely encased. Gently press the pastry
edges to seal in the butter.

4. Turn the pastry parcel 90° clockwise and roll it out again into a
rectangle of a similar size as before, keeping the edges neat. Fold the
bottom third of the rectangle up over the middle third and the top third
down, brushing off any excess flour each time. Lightly press the pastry
edges together, turn the square 90° clockwise, place it in an airtight
container and chill it for 45 minutes.

5. Roll out the dough again on a lightly floured work surface, to a neat
rectangle and fold it into thirds as before. Roll out the dough one last
time and, with one of the short ends nearest to you, fold the top of the
rectangle down to the middle and the bottom edge up to meet it. Turn
the dough 90° clockwise, dust off any excess flour and fold the dough
in half as if closing a book. Place it in an airtight container and chill
for at least 1 hour, or until ready to use.

Continues overleaf

6. Prepare the filling. Tip the rosemary leaves into a bowl. Add the garlic and the fig conserve or chutney and mix to combine.

7. Shape and bake the twists. Dust the work surface with flour and cut the puff pastry block in half. Roll out one half to a neat 40 x 25cm rectangle with one of the short ends nearest to you.

8. Spread the bottom half of the pastry with half of the jam mixture. Lay 4 slices of prosciutto on top of the jam and scatter with half each of the taleggio and parmesan. Season with pepper.

9. Brush the top half of the pastry with beaten egg and fold it over to cover the cheese and prosciutto filling. Gently press the layers together and lightly roll the pastry to neaten, and to compress the filling.

10. Using a pizza wheel or a sharp knife, cut the filled pastry into 12 equal-width vertical strips and brush the top of them with beaten egg. Twist each pastry strip 3 or 4 times and arrange them on a lined baking sheet, leaving space between them. Chill the twists while you repeat with the remaining pastry and filling. Leave in the fridge until the second batch has chilled for a full 30 minutes. Meanwhile, heat the oven to 200°C/180°C fan/Gas 6.

11. Bake the cheese twists for 18–20 minutes, until golden brown and crisp. Leave to cool on the baking sheets and serve at room temperature.

Serves 6
Hands on 1 hour + cooling
Bake 1 hour 20 mins

For the steak filling
2 tbsp olive oil
1 onion, finely chopped
600g braising steak
   or stewing beef
1 tbsp plain flour
350ml beef stock
200ml good ale or hot water
2 bay leaves
½ tsp dried rosemary
1 tbsp dried parsley
100g beef mince (optional)
100g lamb's kidneys,
   trimmed and halved
2 tsp cornflour, mixed
   with 1 tbsp water
salt and freshly ground
   black pepper

For the suet pastry
225g self-raising flour
25g unsalted butter,
   diced and chilled,
   plus extra for greasing
80g beef suet
2–3 tbsp chopped flat-leaf
   parsley (optional)
pinch of salt
5–6 tbsp ice-cold water

YOU WILL NEED
kitchen string
1.2-litre pudding basin,
   greased, then base-lined
   with a disc of baking paper

Steak and kidney pudding

A dish to warm the cockles, this pudding featured a lot in my mum's repertoire when I was a child – from a recipe that goes back through our family for generations. I have departed with tradition to cook the steak-and-kidney filling first, rather than steaming it from raw inside the pastry case, which takes most of the day. I remember vividly my mum calling me to check on the water levels in the pan so that it didn't burn. It's lovely with buttery mash and some good veg – peas and carrots are simply splendid.

1. Make the filling. Heat the olive oil in a large saucepan, add the onion and cook over a medium heat for about 5 minutes, until tender and translucent.

2. Tip the beef into a large mixing bowl, add the flour and season well with salt and pepper, then mix to lightly coat the meat in the flour. Add the beef to the onions, turn up the heat to medium–high and cook the meat, stirring often, for 4–5 minutes, until browned all over.

3. Add the beef stock and ale or hot water and bring to the boil. Add the bay leaves, rosemary, parsley and beef mince (if using), season with salt and pepper, then stir to combine. Cover and cook over a low heat for about 45 minutes, stirring occasionally.

4. Add the kidneys and cook for a further 15 minutes, until cooked through and the beef is tender. Taste and if the beef is still a little tough, continue to cook for a further 5–10 minutes.

5. Spoon half of the cooking liquid into a jug and set aside to make the gravy later. Remove the bay leaves. Gradually, add the cornflour paste to the steak filling and cook, stirring, until the gravy is thick enough to leave a trail that slowly falls back onto itself. Leave the filling to cool.

6. Make the suet pastry. While the filling is cooling, tip the flour into a large mixing bowl and rub in the butter with your fingertips until the mixture resembles breadcrumbs. Lightly rub in the suet, then add the parsley, if using, and salt. Mix in the smaller quantity of ice-cold water with a table knife until the mixture comes together in a firm dough, little by little adding the rest of the water, if needed. Cover the bowl and leave the dough to rest for 10 minutes.

Continues overleaf

7. Measure the basin. I use a length of string and place the basin centrally on top of the string and pull it up either side to calculate how wide the pastry disc needs to be to line the base and sides of the basin.

8. Tip out the dough onto a lightly floured work surface. Cut off about 100g of dough and set it aside to make the lid. Roll out the remaining dough into a neat disc to the measured circumference – for a 1.2-litre pudding basin it should be about 32cm in diameter and 1cm thick. Cut a narrow triangular wedge out of the disc to make it easier to line the basin and add the cut-off piece to the reserved dough for the lid.

9. Press the pastry into the base and up the sides of the basin so it is about 1cm below the rim, pinching the edges together where you cut out the wedge.

10. Roll out the pastry for the lid and cut it into a 15cm disc, using a plate or bowl as a template.

11. Spoon the cooled beef filling into the lined pudding basin, filling it to within 1cm of the top of the pastry. Place the lid directly on top of the filling and within the sides of the pastry lining. Brush a little water around the edge of the lid and, using a small knife or palette knife, fold the sides of the pastry lining over the lid. Smooth the top of the pie and press the sides and lid together using a fork.

12. Cover with a large square of baking paper or foil, so that it overhangs the bowl, and make a pleat down the middle to allow for expansion during cooking. Tie a piece of string around the bowl to secure the paper/foil and to make a handle. Place the bowl in a steamer, cover and gently steam for 1 hour 20 minutes, checking the water levels occasionally and adding more water if needed – don't let it boil dry.

13. Remove the pudding from the steamer, using the string handle to lift it out, and place it on a board or tea towel. Remove the paper/foil, place a plate over the top of the basin and flip it over. Carefully lift off the basin. Use the reserved cooking liquid from the filling to make a gravy to serve with the pudding.

Serves 8–10
Hands on 1 hour + cooling
Bake 35 mins

For the jam
350g strawberries,
    hulled and quartered
150g redcurrants,
    stripped from the stalks
150g raspberries
425g jam sugar
juice of ½ lemon
10g unsalted butter

For the pastry
300g plain flour,
    plus extra for dusting
½ tsp baking powder
pinch of salt
175g unsalted butter,
    chilled and diced
100g caster sugar,
    plus extra for sprinkling
2 eggs, 1 whole, 1 separated
finely grated zest of
    ½ unwaxed lemon
1 tsp lemon juice
2 tsp ice-cold water
icing sugar, for dusting

YOU WILL NEED
sugar thermometer
23cm fluted tart tin
pasta wheel (optional)

Summer berry jam crostata

Jam tarts are so often our bakers' first childhood bakes – scraps of pastry turned into morsels of deliciousness. Here, though, the jam tart is definitely grown up. It gets an Italian twist and becomes a sophisticated crostata with a strawberry, redcurrant and raspberry jam filling and a classic pastry-lattice top. It is equally good enjoyed as a slice after work with a well-earned cup of tea or as a dessert at the end of a Sunday roast.

1. Make the jam. Tip the strawberries, redcurrants and raspberries into a large saucepan with the jam sugar, lemon juice and 2 tablespoons of water. Place the pan over a low heat, stirring often to dissolve the sugar. Bring to the boil and cook, stirring often, for about 30 minutes until the jam reaches setting point (about 105°C on a sugar thermometer).

2. Slide the pan off the heat, add the butter and stir to melt. Pour the jam into a large bowl and leave it to cool completely. Cover and chill in the fridge until needed.

3. Make the pastry. Sift the flour, baking powder and salt into a large mixing bowl. Add the diced butter and, using a table knife, cut the butter into the flour until the pieces are half their original size. Using your fingertips, rub in the butter until the mixture resembles breadcrumbs and there are only very small flecks of butter still visible. Add the sugar.

4. In a small bowl combine 1 whole egg and 1 egg yolk (save the white for glazing), with the lemon zest, lemon juice and iced water.

5. Make a well in the centre of the flour mixture. Add the egg mixture and, using the table knife, combine the dry and wet ingredients until the mixture starts to clump together. Use your hands to gather the pastry into a ball.

6. Divide the pastry into 2 unequal pieces, of two-thirds and one-third. Flatten each portion into a neat disc, then wrap and chill both for 1 hour, until firm.

7. Assemble the tart. Roll out the larger portion of pastry on a lightly floured work surface into a neat disc, 2cm larger all round than the base of the tart tin. Carefully use the disc to line the tin, neatly pressing the dough into the corners and ridges.

Continues overleaf

8. Spoon the jam into the pastry shell and spread it out so that it is 1cm deep – you may not need all the jam (enjoy the remainder on toast).

9. Roll out the remaining pastry on a lightly floured work surface to a disc slightly larger than the top of the tart tin (about 30cm). Cut the dough into 1cm strips, using a pasta wheel or a long knife.

10. Arrange the dough strips in a neat lattice on top of the jam-filled tart, leaving a gap of about 1cm between each strip (see detailed instructions, below). Press the lattice to the sides of the tart shell to stick, then trim the top edge to neaten and chill for 20 minutes.

11. Meanwhile, heat the oven to 180°C/160°C fan/Gas 4 and place a heavy baking sheet on the middle shelf of the oven to heat up.

12. Bake the tart. Brush the lattice and edges of the tart with lightly beaten egg white, sprinkle with caster sugar and bake for about 35 minutes on top of the hot tray until the pastry is golden brown.

13. Leave the tart to cool for 30 minutes in the tin, then transfer it to a wire rack and leave it until cold and the jam has set. Dust with icing sugar to serve.

How to make a pastry lattice

Cover a large baking sheet with a piece of baking paper. Lay one of the longest pastry strips vertically down the middle of the paper. Lay one slightly shorter strip either side of this, leaving a 1cm gap between each strip. Fold the middle strip in half up and back over itself and place another of the longest strips horizontally across the middle. Fold the middle strip back over to cover. Repeat, adding another horizontal strip 1cm beneath the first and this time folding back the first and third vertical strips. Repeat, adding more strips horizontally and vertically, making sure that you keep the lattice even and neat and folding the strips up and over alternately until you have used them all up and the lattice is large enough to cover the top of the tart. Chill the lattice for 20 minutes or freeze it for 10 minutes, until firm but not frozen.

Brush the edges of the tart with water and carefully slide the lattice squarely on top of the tart to cover. Press the edges together to seal and trim off any excess pastry.

Patisserie

Makes 8 buns
Hands on 1 hour 30 mins
+ chilling and rising
Bake 23 mins

For the dough
250g plain flour,
    plus extra for rolling
5g fast-action dried yeast
30g caster sugar
½ tsp salt
100ml whole milk, lukewarm
2 eggs
1 tsp vanilla paste
75g unsalted butter,
    at room temperature

For the custard
200ml whole milk
1 bay leaf
pinch of anise seeds (optional)
1 tsp vanilla paste
40g caster sugar
1 tbsp cornflour
2 egg yolks
pinch of salt

For the filling
200g blackberries
200g blueberries
finely grated zest and juice
    of 1 unwaxed lime
1 tbsp caster sugar
2 tbsp pearl sugar
50g flaked almonds

YOU WILL NEED
2 baking sheets, each lined
    with baking paper
2 oiled proving bags

Blackberry, blueberry and custard brioche buns

Soft and buttery buns filled with decadent custard and tangy autumn berries, with a satisfyingly nutty crunch on top – these are perfect for a late-summer picnic or a weekend sweet brunch. The dough is easier to shape if you prove it overnight in the fridge.

1. Make the dough. Tip the flour into the bowl of a stand mixer fitted with the dough hook. Add the yeast, sugar and salt and use a balloon whisk to combine. Make a well in the centre of the dry ingredients, add the warm milk, 1 egg and the vanilla and mix on low speed until combined. Scrape down the inside of the bowl and continue mixing for about 3 minutes, until the mixture is smooth.

2. With the mixer running on low speed, a spoonful at a time add the butter. Continue mixing for a further 4 minutes, until the dough is silky smooth and elastic and pulls away from the inside of the bowl.

3. Scrape down the inside of the bowl again, cover and leave the dough to rise overnight in the fridge. (Or, if you're intending to bake on the same day, leave the dough at cool room temperature for 1½–2 hours, until doubled in size.)

4. Prepare the custard. While the dough is rising, heat the milk with the bay leaf and anise seeds (if using), the vanilla paste and half the caster sugar, until just below boiling.

5. Meanwhile in a mixing bowl whisk together the remaining sugar, with the cornflour, egg yolks and salt until smooth.

6. Pour the hot milk onto the egg yolks, whisking continuously until smooth. Return the mixture to the pan and cook, whisking continuously over a low heat, for about 1 minute, until the mixture thickens, starts to bubble and you can no longer taste the cornflour. Strain the custard into a clean bowl, cover the surface with baking paper and leave to cool, then chill until you're ready to bake.

7. Shape the dough. Weigh the risen dough and divide it into 8 equal pieces. Using your hands, shape each piece into a taut ball with the seam on the underside.

Continues overleaf

8. Roll each ball on a lightly floured work surface to a 10cm disc. Using your fingers, gently push the middle of each disc to create a nest shape with a 1cm raised border. Place 4 buns on each lined baking sheet, place in an oiled proving bag and leave to prove at room temperature for about 1 hour, until the dough is risen and puffy.

9. Make the filling. Mix the berries in a bowl with the lime zest and juice and the caster sugar.

10. Spoon a rounded tablespoon of custard into the middle of each brioche bun and spread it to the border. Brush the exposed brioche border with the remaining egg and sprinkle with the pearl sugar. Spoon the berry filling onto the custard and scatter with the flaked almonds.

11. Bake the buns for about 23 minutes, until the brioche is golden and the berries are starting to become juicy. Serve warm, or at room temperature.

Makes 16
Hands on 1½ hours
+ resting and chilling
Bake 12–14 mins per batch

For the pastry
175g plain flour, plus
    extra for rolling out
125g strong white bread flour
good pinch of sea salt
2 tsp lemon juice
175g unsalted butter,
    at room temperature
½ tsp ground cinnamon

For the filling
250g caster sugar
5cm cinnamon stick
2 strips of unwaxed lemon zest
1 strip of orange zest
300ml whole milk
40g plain flour
pinch of salt
½ tsp vanilla paste
7 egg yolks

YOU WILL NEED
sugar thermometer
12-hole muffin tins x 2
    (preferably non-stick),
    brushed with melted butter

pastéis de nata

The super-crisp buttery pastry for these special little Portuguese tarts (custard tarts taken to a whole new level) takes time and patience, but is so worth it. Put the radio on and ease into the process – it's an afternoon well spent and with the most satisfyingly crisp and creamy results.

1. Make the pastry. Combine both flours and the pinch of salt in a mixing bowl. Add 150ml of cold water and the lemon juice and use a rubber spatula to bring the ingredients together. Then, use your hands and mix until you have an almost smooth dough (add 1 tablespoon more water, if needed). Cover the mixing bowl with a clean tea towel and leave to rest for 30 minutes.

2. Turn out the dough onto a lightly floured work surface and shape it into a neat square, then roll it into a rectangle three times as long as it is wide – roughly 36 x 12cm. Turn it, if necessary, so that one of the short ends is nearest to you. Try to keep all the sides as neat as possible. Place 125g of the butter between two sheets of baking paper and use a rolling pin to flatten into a 10–11cm square.

3. Place the rolled butter in the middle third of the dough rectangle, then fold the top third down to cover and the bottom third up over that. Press the edges together to seal, turn the square 90° clockwise and, using short, sharp rolling movements, roll the dough out again into a neat rectangle the same size as before. Fold the top third down to the middle again and the bottom third up to cover. Rotate by 90° and repeat. Carefully wrap the dough square in baking paper and chill for 1 hour.

4. Repeat this rolling and folding again twice more so that you will have completed 4 roll and folds. Cover the dough and chill for 1 hour.

5. Soften the remaining 50g of butter so that it is very easily spreadable. Add the cinnamon and mix to combine.

6. Roll out the dough on a lightly floured work surface into a neat 35–40cm square. Using a palette knife, spread the cinnamon butter evenly all over the dough. Roll the dough into a neat, tight spiral log. Cut the log in half, place each half in an airtight container and chill for at least 1 hour, or ideally overnight, until very firm.

Continues overleaf

7. Make the filling. Tip the sugar into a small saucepan over a medium–low heat. Add 150ml of water, the cinnamon stick, and the lemon and orange zests. Bring to the boil to dissolve the sugar, then continue to cook until the syrup reaches 110°C on the sugar thermometer. Remove from the heat.

8. In a medium mixing bowl, whisk 100ml of the milk with all the flour and the pinch of salt until smooth.

9. In a small saucepan heat the remaining 200ml milk to boiling point, then pour the hot milk onto the cold. Add the vanilla and whisk until smooth. Slowly add the hot sugar syrup, whisking continuously, then leave the custard to cool for 10 minutes.

10. Beat the egg yolks together in a medium bowl, and pour in the milk and syrup mixture, whisking until smooth. Strain the custard into a clean jug, then leave until cold before covering and chilling until ready to use.

11. Assemble and bake the tarts. Cut the pastry logs into 16 slices each 1.5cm thick. Place one slice, cut side down, into each hole in the muffin tins, until you have used all the sliced (you won't fill the second tin). Using slightly wet fingers press the pastry discs into the tins, moulding the dough evenly onto the base of the tin and teasing it up the sides to line each hole. Chill for 15 minutes.

12. Meanwhile, heat the oven to its hottest setting – around 240°C/220°C fan/Gas 8, position a shelf in the top third of the oven and place a solid baking sheet on the shelf above that to heat up.

13. Briefly whisk the custard and pour it equally into the pastry cases, filling them three-quarters full. One tray at a time, bake the tarts on the shelf below the hot tray for 12–14 minutes, until the pastry is golden brown and crisp and the custard is set and starting to caramelise on top.

14. Leave the tarts to cool for 1–2 minutes, then remove them from the tin and transfer them to a cooling rack to cool completely. Repeat with the other muffin tin of tarts.

Serves 6
Hands on 2 hours
+ chilling and freezing
Bake 50 mins

For the ice cream
600ml whole milk
150ml double cream
1 vanilla pod, split lengthways
    and seeds scraped
9 large egg yolks
150g caster sugar

For the cheat's rough puff
200g plain flour
pinch of salt
35g unsalted butter,
    cut into cubes and chilled
5–7 tbsp ice-cold water
80g unsalted butter, frozen

For the walnut praline
75g walnut halves or pieces
125g caster sugar
large pinch of sea salt

For the tart
125g caster sugar
50g unsalted butter,
    cut into cubes
4 firm but ripe pears,
    peeled, halved and cored

YOU WILL NEED
cooking thermometer
    (optional)
baking sheet lined with
    a silicone mat
ice-cream machine
25cm heavy-based ovenproof
    frying pan or tart tatin dish

Prue's pear tarte tatin

Sticky caramel and buttery puff pastry with the floral sweetness of perfectly ripe pears. Enjoy the adulation when you turn out a perfect tatin in front of your guests! We're serving it with homemade vanilla ice cream, dotted with walnut praline, for extra scoops of comfort.

1. Make the ice cream. Start by making a crème anglaise. Heat the milk, cream and vanilla seeds in a saucepan over a medium heat to just below boiling point. Remove from the heat and leave to stand.

2. In a large bowl, using an electric hand whisk, whisk the egg yolks and caster sugar until thick and pale, and the mixture leaves a ribbon trail when you lift the whisk. Pour in the warmed milk mixture, whisking continuously. Return the mixture to the pan and cook over a very low heat for 3–4 minutes, whisking continuously, until smooth and thick enough to coat the back of a spoon. The temperature should read 83°C on a cooking thermometer when the crème anglaise is ready. Remove the pan from the heat and pass the crème anglaise through a sieve into a clean bowl, then place the bowl in an ice bath and leave to cool.

3. Make the cheat's rough puff. Mix the flour and salt together in a mixing bowl. Using your fingertips, rub in the chilled butter until the mixture resembles fine breadcrumbs. Gradually mix in the ice-cold water – using just enough for the mixture to come together in a ball of dough.

4. Roll out the dough on a lightly floured work surface into a 30 x 10cm rectangle. With one of the short ends nearest to you, coarsely grate half of the frozen butter over the bottom two-thirds of the dough. Fold down the top third and fold up the bottom third as if folding a letter. Turn the folded dough through 90° and roll it out into a rectangle the same size as before. Repeat this process, adding the remaining frozen butter and folding as before. Place the dough in an airtight container and leave to rest in the fridge for 30 minutes.

5. Repeat this rolling and folding process twice more, without adding butter, chilling the pastry for 30 minutes each time.

6. Make the walnut praline. While the pastry is chilling, spread out the walnuts on a baking sheet and toast them in the oven for 8–10 minutes, until dark golden. Remove from the oven and set aside.

Continues overleaf

7. Meanwhile, heat the caster sugar in a saucepan over a medium heat, until the sugar melts to a golden caramel, swirling the pan from time to time. Add the walnuts to the pan and swirl them around to coat them in the syrup, then pour the praline onto one half of the baking sheet lined with the silicone mat. Sprinkle with sea salt. Fold the other half of the silicone mat over the walnut praline while it is still warm, then, with a rolling pin, roll out the praline flat. Leave the praline to cool and set hard, then peel off the mat and roughly chop the praline into small (but not fine) pieces.

8. Finish the ice cream. Pour the cooled crème anglaise into an ice-cream machine and churn for 20–25 minutes, until it is soft set. Just before the ice cream is ready, add the walnut praline. Scrape the ice cream into an ice-cream container and freeze for 30 minutes, until firm.

9. Heat the oven to 200°C/180°C fan/Gas 6.

10. Make the tart. Tip the sugar into the frying pan or tatin dish and place it over a medium heat. Cook until the sugar melts to a golden caramel, swirling from time to time.

11. Add the butter to the pan, stirring until combined. Add the pear halves and spoon the buttery caramel over the pears. Reduce the heat and simmer for 5 minutes, until the pears are tender but retain their shape. Remove the pan from the heat, then lift the pears out of the pan onto a plate lined with kitchen paper. Leave to cool slightly.

12. Carefully pour most of the caramel into a heatproof jug, leaving just a thin layer on the base of the pan. Arrange the pears cut-side up with their pointy ends meeting in the middle of the pan.

13. Roll out the pastry on a lightly floured work surface to about 5mm thick. Cut out a disc slightly larger than the frying pan or tatin dish. Roll the pastry onto your rolling pin, then unroll it over the pears to cover evenly. Carefully tuck the edges of the pastry into the sides of the pan and prick the surface with a fork. Bake for 35–40 minutes, until the pastry is puffed up and golden, and the caramel is bubbling around the sides.

14. Remove the tatin from the oven and leave it to cool for 5 minutes. Meanwhile, reheat the reserved caramel. Carefully invert the tart onto a serving plate and spoon over the warmed reserved caramel. Serve cut into slices with scoops of the ice cream.

Makes 24
Hands on 30 mins
+ resting and cooling
Bake 13 mins

For the madeleines
160g unsalted butter
3 eggs
150g caster sugar
finely grated zest of
    ½ unwaxed lemon
1 tsp vanilla paste
150g plain flour
1 tsp baking powder
pinch of salt

To decorate
150g white chocolate,
    chopped
150g 70% dark chocolate,
    chopped

YOU WILL NEED
12-hole madeleine tins x 2,
    well-greased with butter
    and lightly dusted with flour
large piping bag
cooking thermometer

Chocolate madeleines

Arrive at a friend's with a gift of these in hand and you will definitely be welcome to come again! They are extra-special for being dipped in dark chocolate, with a white-chocolate swirl. The madeleines will rise best if you make the mixture the day before you intend to bake.

1. Make the batter. Melt the butter either in a small saucepan or in the microwave and set aside.

2. Using a balloon whisk, in a bowl beat together the eggs and sugar for 1 minute, until foamy. Add the lemon zest and vanilla and mix again. Sift the flour, baking powder and salt into the bowl and lightly mix to combine. Add the melted butter and beat again until smooth. Scrape down the inside of the bowl, cover and chill for at least 6 hours, or ideally overnight.

3. Pop the prepared madeleine tins in the fridge for 10 minutes and heat the oven to 200°C/180°C fan/Gas 6.

4. Bake the madeleines. Scoop the madeleine mixture into a piping bag, snip the end, and pipe it into the chilled madeleine tins, filling them to just below the rim.

5. Place the trays in the oven and immediately lower the oven temperature to 180°C/160°C fan/Gas 4. Bake the madeleines for 12–13 minutes, until well risen and golden.

6. Leave the madeleines in the tins for 1–2 minutes, then carefully remove them from the moulds and transfer them to a wire rack to cool completely. Wash and thoroughly dry the madeleine tins.

7. Decorate the madeleines. Tip 100g of the white chocolate into a heatproof bowl. Using a separate heatproof bowl, repeat for the dark chocolate. Melt each portion of chocolate over a pan of barely simmering water, stirring until smooth, until the white chocolate reaches 45–50°C on the thermometer and the dark chocolate is 50–55°C.

8. Remove the bowls from the heat (but leave the water bubbling away) and add the remaining 50g of matching chopped chocolate to each bowl. Stir until melted and smooth. Leave the white chocolate to cool to 26–27°C and the dark chocolate to 28–29°C.

Continues overleaf

9. Return the bowls to the pans of water and, stirring, reheat until the white chocolate reaches 28–29°C and the dark chocolate reaches 31–32°C – this will take only a matter of moments. (The precise tempering is important for a perfectly glossy finish.)

10. Drizzle a teaspoon of white chocolate into each mould in the madeleine tin followed by a teaspoon of dark chocolate. Using a skewer or teaspoon, marble the chocolates together and then press one madeleine into each pool of chocolate, shell-shape down.

11. Place the tins in the fridge for 5–10 minutes to set the chocolate, by which time the chocolate will have hardened and the madeleines should pop cleanly out of the tins, ready to serve or to parcel up for gifting.

Makes 8
Hands on 1½ hours
+ resting and cooling
Bake 38 mins

For the pastry
150g unsalted butter,
    at room temperature
50g icing sugar, sifted,
    plus extra for dusting
2 egg yolks
1 tsp vanilla extract
300g plain flour
1–2 tbsp double cream
pinch of salt

For the filling
125g unsalted butter,
    at room temperature
125g caster sugar
1 tsp vanilla extract
2 eggs
finely grated zest of
    ½ unwaxed lemon
75g ground almonds
50g ground pistachios
2 tsp plain flour
pinch of salt
2 tbsp apricot jam

For the honey cream
4 tbsp runny honey
300ml double cream

To decorate
8 fresh figs, each cut
    into sixths
120g raspberries

YOU WILL NEED
8–9cm tartlet moulds or
    rings x 8 (about 2cm deep)
baking beans or rice
2 large piping bags, one
    fitted with a medium
    open star nozzle

Fig and raspberry tarts with burnt honey cream

These would not look out of place in a French pâtissérie window – the ultimate temptation for anyone with a penchant for a crème anglaise and fruit tart. Burnt honey cream adds a warm twist here, and is a wonderful pairing for grassy pistachios and sweet figs and raspberries.

1. Make the pastry. Beat the butter and icing sugar in a stand mixer fitted with the beater, on medium speed for about 2 minutes, until pale and creamy. Add the egg yolks and vanilla and mix again until combined.

2. Scrape down the inside of the bowl using a rubber spatula and add the flour, 1 tablespoon of double cream and the salt and mix again until the dough starts to clump together – be careful not to overwork the dough. Add a little more cream, if needed.

3. Tip out the dough onto the work surface and lightly knead it to bring it together into a neat ball. Flatten it into a disc, place it in an airtight container and chill it for at least 1 hour, until firm.

4. Lightly dust the work surface with flour and divide the dough into 8 equal pieces. Roll out each piece into a neat 13–14cm-diameter disc, about 2mm thick, and use the discs to line the tart moulds, gently pressing the pastry into the base and up the sides and leaving any excess overhanging the edge. Chill for 30 minutes, until firm.

5. Heat the oven to 180°C/160°C fan/Gas 4.

6. Trim the excess pastry from the top of each tart and prick the base with a fork. Line each pastry case with foil and fill it with baking beans or rice. Bake for about 20 minutes, until pale golden. Carefully remove the foil and beans or rice and bake the cases for a further 2 minutes to dry out the bases, then leave them to cool slightly.

7. Make the filling. While the pastry cases are cooling, beat the butter, caster sugar and vanilla in a stand mixer fitted with the beater, on medium speed for about 2 minutes, until pale and creamy. One at a time, add the eggs, beating well between each addition.

Continues overleaf

8. Mix in the lemon zest, then add the ground almonds, pistachios, flour and salt. Beat until smooth, then cover and set the frangipane aside at room temperature until needed.

9. Warm the apricot jam in a small saucepan and lightly brush it over the base of each tart. Scoop the frangipane into the piping bag without the nozzle, pipe it equally into the tarts and spread it level (alternatively, you can just spoon the frangipane into the cases, if you prefer).

10. Bake the tarts for about 18 minutes, until the frangipane is just set and the cases are golden brown. Leave to cool to room temperature.

11. Make the honey cream. While the tarts are baking, warm the honey in a small saucepan over a medium–low heat until runny. Stirring continuously, cook the honey for about 2 minutes, until it just starts to caramelise – be careful not to let it burn. Remove the pan from the heat and stir in half the cream. If the honey hardens, return the pan to a very low heat and stir until it melts again. Pour the honey cream into a bowl, leave it to cool, then chill until needed.

12. Finish the tarts. Whisk the remaining cream into the honey cream with a balloon whisk until it holds stiff peaks. Scoop it into the piping bag fitted with the medium star nozzle and pipe a swirl on top of each tart. Arrange the figs and raspberries on top of the cream, then dust with icing sugar and serve.

Serves 8
Hands on 1 hour
+ chilling and freezing
Bake 1¼ hours

For the pie crust
250g plain flour
¾ tsp salt
165g unsalted butter,
    cubed and chilled
1 tbsp cider vinegar
5 tbsp ice-cold water

For the butternut custard
220g butternut squash purée
    (see directions, overleaf)
150g dark brown soft sugar
2 eggs, lightly beaten
150ml double cream,
    plus 300ml extra to serve
40ml whole milk
1 tbsp vanilla extract
1 tsp cornflour
2 tsp ground cinnamon
½ tsp ground allspice
½ tsp freshly grated nutmeg
½ tsp ground cardamom
¼ tsp freshly ground
    black pepper
¼ tsp ground cloves
¼ tsp ground ginger
¾ tsp salt

For the maple pecan streusel
130g pecans, roughly chopped
30g unsalted butter, melted
60g dark brown soft sugar
4 tbsp maple syrup
1 tbsp plain flour
1 tsp ground cinnamon
½ tsp salt

YOU WILL NEED
round metal pie dish
    (about 4cm deep)
    with a 20cm base
baking beans or rice

BAKER'S RECIPE

Spiced butternut pie with maple pecan streusel

Pies like this are a bit unconventional in the UK, but they are delicious and I think we need to appreciate them more! This one embodies everything I love about autumn, my favourite time to get baking. I have made it a tradition to bake the pies for my family when winter squashes are in season.

1. Make the pie crust. Mix the flour and salt in a large mixing bowl. Rub the butter into the flour using your fingertips until there are still visible pea-sized lumps of butter in the flour. Add the vinegar and water, then mix with your hands until the pastry just starts to come together in a shaggy dough, making sure you don't overmix it. Flatten the dough into a rough disc, then wrap and chill it for at least 30 minutes.

2. Make the butternut custard. While the crust is chilling, in a large bowl, whisk the butternut purée, sugar and eggs with a balloon whisk until just combined. Add the cream, milk, vanilla, cornflour, spices and salt and mix to combine. Do not overmix – you want to avoid incorporating air and the mixture bubbling.

3. Gently roll out the chilled pie-crust dough on a lightly floured work surface to a 35cm-diameter circle, about 4mm thick and large enough to line the dish. Press the pastry into the base and up the sides of the dish, leaving a 2cm overhang, then trim any excess. Tuck the overhang under itself to create a smooth, thick edge, then crimp by pressing your thumb into the dough and pinching around it. Place the lined dish in the freezer for 15 minutes to firm up.

4. Heat the oven to 190°C/170°C fan/Gas 5.

5. Line the pie crust with foil, fill it with baking beans or rice and blind bake for about 25 minutes, until the edges start to turn golden. Remove the foil and beans or rice, prick the base with a fork and bake for a further 5 minutes to cook the base.

6. Bake the filling. Pour the butternut custard into the cooked crust and bake for 30–35 minutes, until the filling puffs up slightly at the edges, but the centre still wobbles.

Continues overleaf

7. Make the pecan streusel. While the filling is baking, mix together all the streusel ingredients in a bowl until combined.

8. Finish the pie. Remove the pie from the oven and carefully spoon the pecan streusel over the top in an even layer. Return the pie to the oven for 15 minutes, until the pecans brown slightly and the centre of the pie barely wobbles – do not overbake it. Leave the pie to cool, then chill for at least 4 hours, ideally overnight, to set.

9. Let the pie come to room temperature before serving. Lightly whip the extra cream to soft peaks and add a dollop to each slice of pie to serve.

How to make butternut purée

To make 220g of butternut purée, you will need ½ medium–large butternut squash, peeled, deseeded, and cut into chunks. Roast in an oven, preheated to 200°C/180°C fan/Gas 6, or steam the squash until soft and tender when pricked with a fork. Purée the squash with a hand blender or food processor until completely smooth, then leave to cool.

Makes 24
Hands on 2 hours
+ infusing and chilling
Bake 50 mins

**For the vanilla
coffee custard**
400ml whole milk
20g coffee beans
½ vanilla pod, split lengthways
120g caster sugar
4 egg yolks
2 tbsp cornflour

For the craquelin
50g unsalted butter, softened
50g light brown soft sugar
50g plain flour
25g flaked almonds,
    very finely chopped
pinch of salt
2 tbsp icing sugar, sifted,
    plus extra for dusting

For the choux pastry
100ml whole milk
75g unsalted butter, at room
    temperature, diced
1 tsp caster sugar
pinch of salt
125g plain flour, sifted
4 eggs, lightly beaten

For the tuiles
40g unsalted butter
2 tsp runny honey
50g caster sugar
30g plain flour
25g cocoa nibs
25g flaked almonds,
    finely chopped
pinch of salt

For the blackcurrant filling
300g blackcurrants
50g caster sugar
juice of ¼ lemon
300ml double cream

Continues overleaf

'Fallen angel' profiteroles

*These elegant choux delights are topped with a creamy blackcurrant
compôte and filled with a custard cream that is delicately infused with
coffee. They are decadent and indulgent – and so good! Why have we called
them fallen angels? Because they are the epitome of naughty but nice!*

1. Make the vanilla coffee custard. Heat the milk with the coffee
beans and vanilla in a small pan until just boiling, then remove from
the heat and leave to infuse for 1 hour. Strain the milk through a sieve
to remove the beans. Return the infused milk to the pan, add half the
caster sugar to the infused milk and reheat until just boiling.

2. In a mixing bowl, whisk the remaining 60g of sugar, the egg yolks
and the cornflour until smooth and creamy. Whisking continuously,
pour the hot milk into the bowl and whisk until smooth. Pour the
mixture back into the pan and whisk over a low heat until the sauce
starts to bubble and thicken. Continue to cook, stirring continuously,
for about 1 minute to cook out the cornflour. Strain the custard into
a clean bowl, cover the surface to prevent a skin forming and leave
to cool. Once cooled, chill for at least 4 hours.

3. Make the craquelin. In a small bowl, beat the butter with the brown
sugar with a wooden spoon until smooth. Beat in the flour, chopped
almonds and salt until smooth. Flatten the mixture into a disc and roll
it between two sheets of baking paper into a thin layer, about 1–2mm
thick, then chill for 30 minutes or freeze for 5 minutes.

4. Heat the oven to 190°C/170°C fan/Gas 5.

5. Make the choux pastry. Heat the milk, 100ml of water, and the butter,
caster sugar and salt in a saucepan over a medium heat. Stir to melt the
butter, then bring to a rolling boil. Remove from the heat and quickly
add the flour. Using a wooden spoon, beat vigorously until the batter is
smooth, then return the pan to a low heat, stirring for 20–30 seconds,
until the mixture is glossy and cleanly leaves the sides of the pan.

6. Tip the choux mixture into a large mixing bowl and leave it to cool
for 5 minutes. Gradually beat in the eggs, mixing well until the batter
is silky smooth and reluctantly drops off the spoon. (You might not
need to add the last 2–3 teaspoons of egg.)

Continues overleaf

'Fallen angel' profiteroles (continued)

YOU WILL NEED
large piping bag fitted with
a medium plain nozzle
2 baking sheets, each lined
with baking paper
4cm plain round cutter
large piping bag fitted with
a medium star nozzle

7. Scoop the mixture into the large piping bag fitted with the medium plain nozzle. Pipe 24 mounds, each about 1 tablespoon, of the choux mixture onto the lined baking sheets.

8. Using the 4cm plain cutter, stamp out 24 discs from the chilled craquelin and place a disc on top of each choux-pastry mound. Dust with the 2 tablespoons of icing sugar and bake for 25–30 minutes, until well risen, deep golden brown and crisp. Leave to cool.

9. Make the tuiles. Melt the butter with the honey and caster sugar in a small saucepan over a medium–low heat. Remove from the heat and cool for 3–4 minutes before adding the flour, cocoa nibs, flaked almonds and salt. Mix until everything is thoroughly combined, then chill the mixture in the pan for 30 minutes, until firm.

10. Heat the oven to 170°C/150°C fan/Gas 3. Re-line one of the baking sheets with baking paper.

11. Roll the tuile mixture into 20 cherry-sized balls and place 6 or 7 at a time, spaced well apart, on the re-lined baking sheet. Bake the tuiles in batches for about 6–7 minutes each, until golden brown and bubbling. Remove from the oven, then leave to cool and harden on the baking sheet. When cool, break each tuile in half.

12. Make the blackcurrant filling. Tip the blackcurrants into a small saucepan, add the caster sugar and lemon juice and cook, stirring often, over a medium–low heat until the fruit is soft and jammy (about 3–5 minutes). Leave the compôte to cool.

13. Whisk the double cream until it holds stiff peaks. Spoon 3 tablespoons of the whipped cream into a separate bowl and mix in 1 tablespoon of the cooled blackcurrant compôte.

14. Whisk the chilled custard until smooth and fold in the remaining whipped cream. Scoop the mixture into the large piping bag fitted with the medium star nozzle.

15. Assemble the profiteroles. Cut the top off each choux bun and spoon a teaspoonful of the remaining blackcurrant compôte into the bottom of each. Pipe the custard mixture into the buns to fill and put the lids back on. Spoon or pipe the blackcurrant cream on top and decorate each bun with half a tuile and a final dusting of icing sugar.

Makes 8
Hands on 2 hours + resting, chilling and proving
Bake 27 mins

For the dough
500g strong white bread flour
15g caster sugar
7g fast-action dried yeast
1 tsp salt
150ml whole milk
2 tsp lemon juice
275g unsalted butter, chilled
1 egg, beaten, to glaze

For the mac 'n' cheese
50g unsalted butter
50g plain flour
500ml whole milk
1 bay leaf
2 tsp Dijon mustard
½ tsp cayenne pepper
200g mature cheddar, grated
1 tbsp finely chopped
 flat-leaf parsley
150g dried macaroni pasta
5 rashers of smoked
 streaky bacon
salt and freshly ground
 black pepper
100g parmesan,
 finely grated, to serve

YOU WILL NEED
lightly oiled tray or plastic box
baking tray, lined with
 baking paper
pizza wheel
2 baking sheets, each lined
 with baking paper

Mac 'n' cheese Danish pastries

The dough for these double-carb, cheesy-umami, and (frankly) totally heavenly pastries is best when made slowly with an overnight rest after you have completed the roll-and-folds. Then, you can do the final assembly in the morning and the pastries will be ready to serve at lunchtime.

1. Make the dough. Combine the flour, sugar, yeast and salt in the bowl of a stand mixer fitted with a dough hook. Heat the milk with 160ml of water until lukewarm, add the lemon juice and 25g of the butter to the liquid and leave for 30 seconds to soften the butter. Pour the warm milk mixture into the mixer bowl and mix on medium–low speed to combine. Scrape down the inside of the bowl, then mix again for about 3 minutes, until the dough is nearly smooth – it should not be elastic at this stage, but the ingredients should be thoroughly combined.

2. Turn out the dough and shape it into a 20cm square. Place the square in the lightly oiled tray (or plastic box), cover and chill for 3–4 hours.

3. Prepare the mac 'n' cheese. While the dough is chilling, melt the 50g butter in a small saucepan over a medium heat. Add the flour and cook for 1 minute, stirring continuously. Slowly pour in the milk, whisking all the time until smooth. Add the bay leaf, mustard and cayenne and bring to the boil. Reduce the heat and simmer very gently for about 5 minutes, until smooth and thickened, stirring occasionally.

4. Remove the pan from the heat, then add the cheddar and parsley. Mix until the cheese is melted and smooth and season well with salt and pepper. Remove the bay leaf, cover the surface of the sauce with baking paper to prevent a skin forming, and leave until cold.

5. Bring a large pan of salted water to the boil. Add the macaroni, stir to separate the pasta and cook for 1 minute less than the suggested cooking time on the packet, or until al dente. Drain and cool thoroughly under cold running water. Leave the pasta to drain well.

6. Add the pasta to the cheese sauce and mix to combine. Cover and chill until you're ready to assemble the pastries (overnight is fine).

7. Laminate and prove the dough. Cut the remaining 250g butter into quarters and lay the butter slices side by side on a sheet of baking paper. Cover with more paper, then use a rolling pin to press and roll the butter into a neat 16cm square. Cover and chill for 30 minutes.

Continues overleaf

8. Roll out the chilled dough on a lightly floured work surface to a neat 50 x 18cm rectangle and with a short side nearest you. Place the chilled butter in the middle of the dough and fold the top third of the dough over the butter to cover, brush off any excess flour and fold the bottom third up over the top. Press the sides to seal the butter in a dough parcel.

9. Turn the dough parcel 90° and flour the work surface. Starting at the middle of the dough and using a short, sharp tapping action with the rolling pin, flatten and then gently roll the dough into a neat 50 x 18cm rectangle, keeping the sides and ends neat and straight.

10. Fold the top third of the dough down to the middle, brush off any excess flour and fold the bottom third up to cover. Turn the dough through 90° and repeat this rolling and folding once more, then wrap the dough parcel and place it in the fridge for 1 hour to relax the gluten in the flour and firm up the butter.

11. Repeat this rolling and folding two more times so that you have made 4 turns in total. Place the dough on the lined baking tray, then cover and chill overnight.

12. Shape the dough. Unwrap the dough and cut it in half. On a lightly floured work surface, roll out one half to a neat 11 x 42cm rectangle. Using the pizza wheel, trim the edges and then cut the rectangle into four 10cm squares (they don't need to be perfect) and place each one on a lined baking sheet. Repeat with the second half of the dough.

13. Using the point of a sharp knife, score a 1cm border all around each dough square. Cover loosely and leave at room temperature for about 1 hour, until risen to almost double the height.

14. Finish the mac 'n' cheese. Heat the oven to 200°C/180°C fan/Gas 6, then place the bacon in a foil-lined baking tray and cook for about 10 minutes, until crisp. Cut the cooked bacon into small pieces and stir the pieces into the mac 'n' cheese.

15. Assemble the pastries. Brush the border of each pastry with beaten egg and bake for 12 minutes, until risen and golden. Carefully cut along the score marks and discard the square middle layer from each pastry. Spoon the mac 'n' cheese into the middle of each pastry to fill, then bake for a further 12–15 minutes, until bubbling and golden brown.

16. Scatter generously with freshly grated parmesan to serve.

Makes 8
Hands on 30 mins + cooling
Bake 2 hours 5 minutes

For the meringues
150g caster sugar
4 egg whites
pinch of cream of tartar
pinch of salt
½ tsp vanilla paste
100g light muscovado sugar
50g flaked almonds

For the plums
800g ripe plums (about 12),
    halved and stones removed
1 cinnamon stick
1 vanilla pod,
    split lengthways
2 star anise
juice of 1 orange
2 tbsp runny honey
    or maple syrup
2 tbsp light muscovado sugar

For the chai-spiced cream
400ml double cream
½ tsp ground cinnamon
¼ tsp ground cardamom
good pinch of freshly
    grated nutmeg
good pinch of ground allspice
3 pieces of stem ginger in
    syrup, finely chopped
2 tbsp stem ginger syrup

YOU WILL NEED
large baking sheet lined
    with baking paper
medium roasting tin,
    baking tin or ovenproof
    dish, lined with
    baking paper

Roasted plum brown-sugar meringues

Making meringues with brown and toasted white sugar gives them a toffee-like depth of flavour, and a lovely texture that's chewier than just white-sugar meringues. Make these the day before you plan to serve them.

1. Heat the oven to 190°C/170°C fan/Gas 5.

2. Make the meringues. Tip the caster sugar into a small roasting tin and place it in the oven for 5 minutes, until hot. Remove the sugar from the oven and turn the heat down to 120°C/100°C fan/Gas ¾.

3. While the sugar is warming, whisk the egg whites with the cream of tartar and salt in a stand mixer fitted with the whisk, on medium speed for 2 minutes, until they hold soft peaks. Tip all the hot caster sugar into the egg whites. Add the vanilla and whisk for about 3 minutes, until the hot sugar has dissolved and the meringue is very stiff and glossy.

4. A tablespoon at a time, add the muscovado, whisking continuously. Whisk for a further 2–3 minutes, until the muscovado is incorporated. Rub a little of the mixture between your finger and thumb, it should be silky smooth with no graininess; if not, mix for another minute or so.

5. Shape and bake the meringues. Using a large metal spoon, pile the meringue into 8 individual mounds, each about 10cm in diameter, on the lined baking sheet. Make an indent in the middle of each one with the back of a spoon and scatter with the flaked almonds. Bake on the middle shelf for 1½ hours, until crisp. Turn off the oven and leave the meringues inside to cool with the door ajar for at least 2 hours or overnight.

6. Make the plum filling. Mix the plums in a large bowl with the cinnamon stick, split vanilla pod, star anise, orange juice, honey (or maple syrup) and sugar until combined. Leave to sit at room temperature for 30 minutes, then heat the oven to 180°C/160°C fan/Gas 4.

7. Arrange the plums, cut-side up, in a single layer in the lined roasting tin (or equivalent). Add any residual juice and the spices and bake for about 30 minutes, until the plums are very tender and starting to caramelise at the edges (the timing will depend on ripeness), then leave to cool.

8. Make the chai-spiced cream. While the filling is cooling, whisk the cream in a mixing bowl with the rest of the ingredients using a balloon whisk until thickened and the cream holds firm peaks.

9. Assemble the dessert. Arrange the meringues on serving plates and top with a generous spoonful of the chai-spiced cream. Top with the roasted plums, drizzle with the pan juices, and serve.

Dessert

Serves 10–12
Hands on 1 hour + cooling
Bake 1½ hours

**For the roasted
strawberry cream**
400g strawberries, hulled
30g caster sugar
1 vanilla pod, split and
    seeds scraped out
500ml double cream

For the meringue
6 egg whites
pinch of cream of tartar
pinch of salt
350g caster sugar
1 tsp vanilla paste
1 tsp white wine vinegar
1 tsp cornflour
50g flaked almonds

To serve
200g raspberries
200g blueberries
250g strawberries,
    hulled and quartered
icing sugar, sifted

YOU WILL NEED
medium roasting tin lined
    with baking paper
large baking sheet lined
    with baking paper

Summer berry sheet pavlova

*A summer spectacular and perennial crowd-pleaser, this pavlova requires no
fancy shaping or tins – simply spoon it into a rectangle on a baking sheet and
bake. The roasted strawberry cream showcases the best of British summer
fruit. Feel free to add fresh redcurrants, if they are available, and perhaps
embellish the pavlova with rose petals or other edible flowers.*

1. Heat the oven to 200°C/180°C fan/Gas 6.

2. Make the roasted strawberry cream. Tip the strawberries and sugar
into a mixing bowl, then add the vanilla seeds and mix to combine.
Tip everything into the lined roasting tin and roast the strawberries
for 20–25 minutes, until very soft, juicy and just starting to caramelise
at the edges. Leave to cool.

3. Reduce the oven to 150°C/130°C fan/Gas 2 and place a baking sheet
on the middle shelf to heat up at the same time.

4. Make the meringue. Whisk the egg whites, cream of tartar and salt
in a stand mixer fitted with a whisk, on medium speed for 3 minutes, to
soft peaks. A spoonful at a time, add the sugar, mixing continuously on
medium–high speed, then mix for 5–10 minutes, until very thick, glossy
and white, and you can feel no grains of sugar if you rub the meringue
between your fingers. If there are, whisk for 1 minute more and check
again. Add the vanilla and mix to combine. In a small bowl, combine the
vinegar and cornflour. Add this to the meringue; whisk for 20 seconds.

5. Spoon the meringue mixture onto the lined baking sheet in mounds,
forming it into a 30 x 20cm rectangle. Scatter the flaked almonds around
the edge. Slide the baking sheet into the oven on top of the hot one inside
and lower the oven to 120°C/100°C fan/Gas ¾. Bake for 1 hour, until the
meringue is crisp on the outside and marshmallowy in the middle. Turn
off the oven and leave the meringue inside to cool with the oven door
closed for 1 hour and then leave the door ajar until completely cold.

6. Remove the meringue from the oven and carefully slide it off the
paper onto a board or serving platter.

7. Whizz the roasted strawberries and all the juices in a blender to a
smooth purée. Whip the cream to soft, floppy peaks, then lightly fold in
three-quarters of the purée so that it is marbled throughout the cream.

8. Spoon the cream into the centre of the pavlova in pillowy mounds.
Drizzle over the remaining purée and arrange the raspberries, blueberries
and quartered strawberries on top. Dust with icing sugar, to serve.

Prue's spotted dick and custard

Serves 6
Hands on 1 hour
Steam 1½ hours

For the spotted dick
125g currants
finely grated zest and
   juice of 1 orange
finely grated zest and juice
   of 1 unwaxed lemon
½ tsp bicarbonate of soda
300g plain flour
2 tsp ground cinnamon
2 tsp baking powder
150g shredded vegetable suet
75g light brown soft sugar
200ml whole milk
just-boiled water,
   for steaming

For the syrup
200g caster sugar
100ml just-boiled water
1 lemon wedge

For the custard
250ml whole milk
250ml double cream
½ vanilla pod, split
   and seeds scraped
6 large egg yolks
50g caster sugar

YOU WILL NEED
1-litre pudding basin,
   greased
kitchen string

The original old-school nursery pudding, there is no lumpy custard here! The world 'dick' is a shortening of the medieval English 'puddick', meaning pudding. And the spots, of course, are the scattering of dried fruit throughout. We're using vegetable suet here, to make this pudding veggie-friendly, and Prue's custard is made using double cream as well as milk, for spoonfuls of extra luxury.

1. Make the spotted dick. Tip the currants into a medium heatproof bowl. Add the orange juice and lemon juice and stir together. Cover the bowl with a saucer and place the bowl in a microwave on its highest power for 3 minutes. Remove the bowl from the microwave, remove the saucer, then stir in the bicarbonate of soda and leave the currants to stand for 15 minutes, until plumped up. Alternatively, if you don't have a microwave, tip the currants, orange and lemon juice into a small saucepan over a medium heat and bring the liquid to the boil. Remove from the heat, stir in the bicarbonate of soda and leave the fruit to soak for 3 hours, until plump. Drain the currants through a sieve.

2. Place the flour, cinnamon, baking powder, vegetable suet, brown sugar, orange zest, lemon zest and drained currants into a mixing bowl and mix with a balloon whisk to combine. Add the milk and stir with a wooden spoon to make a soft dough.

3. Spoon the mixture into the buttered basin. Lay a sheet of foil over a sheet of non-stick baking paper (these need to be large enough to cover the top of the pudding bowl). Pick up both and fold a vertical pleat down the centre. Place the foil and paper over the top of the bowl, positioning the pleat down the centre.

4. Tie a piece of string around the edge of the bowl to secure the foil and paper, then tie the string over the top of the bowl and secure it on the other side to make a handle.

5. Place a side plate upside down in the bottom of a large, lidded saucepan and place the pudding basin on top of the plate. Fill the pan two-thirds of the way up with just-boiled water.

6. Cover the pan with the lid, place it on a medium–high heat and bring the water back to the boil. Then, reduce the heat and simmer for 1½ hours, until the foil top has risen a bit and the pleat is stretched slightly.

Continues overleaf

7. Make the syrup. While the pudding is steaming, tip 50g of the caster sugar into a small saucepan and add 3 tablespoons of cold water. Place the pan over a low heat and stir until the sugar dissolves, then increase the heat to medium and cook to a golden caramel.

8. Remove the pan from the heat and very carefully pour in the just-boiled water (stand back as the caramel will spit a bit). Return the pan to a low heat, add the lemon wedge and remaining 150g of caster sugar, and stir until the mixture comes to the boil. Reduce the heat to its lowest setting and simmer very gently for 20 minutes, until the mixture becomes a light golden colour and has a syrup consistency. Remove the pan from the heat again and set aside until ready to use.

9. Make the custard. Place the milk, cream and vanilla seeds into a pan and bring the liquid to a simmer.

10. Place the egg yolks and sugar into a bowl and whisk together until combined. A little at a time, pour the warm milk mixture onto the eggs, stirring continuously with a balloon whisk. Pour the mixture back into the pan and cook over a low heat, stirring with a wooden spatula, until the custard is just thickened.

11. Once the steaming time is up, use the string handle to carefully remove the pudding basin from the pan. Leave it to cool for 3 minutes, then remove the string, foil and baking paper.

12. Place a serving plate over the top of the basin, then carefully turn out the pudding onto the plate. Re-warm the syrup and pour it over, and serve with the custard.

Serves 8–10
Hands on 1 hour + chilling
Bake 1 hour 10 mins

For the pastry
110g unsalted butter, softened
50g icing sugar, sifted
2 egg yolks
200g plain flour
2 tsp double cream
pinch of salt
1 egg white, lightly beaten

For the filling
finely grated zest and juice
    of 3 unwaxed lemons
2 large passion fruit, halved
    and pulp scooped out
200g caster sugar
7 eggs
pinch of salt
175ml double cream

To serve
2 tbsp icing sugar, for glazing
crème fraîche
2 passion fruit, halved and
    pulp scooped out (optional)

YOU WILL NEED
23cm loose-bottomed fluted
    tart tin (about 3.5cm deep)
baking beans or rice
kitchen blowtorch

Lemon and passion fruit brûlée tart

This summer crowd-pleaser has a satisfying crunch that gives way to a tangy, lemon-custard and passion-fruit filling in a perfect balance of sharp and sweet. Serve it with a bowl of crème fraîche for spooning over and perhaps an extra drizzle of passion-fruit pulp.

1. Make the pastry. Beat the butter and icing sugar in a stand mixer fitted with the beater, on medium speed for 3–4 minutes, until pale and creamy. Add the egg yolks and mix again until combined. Scrape down the inside of the bowl using a rubber spatula and add the flour, cream and salt. Mix slowly until the dough starts to clump together.

2. Tip out the dough onto the work surface and lightly knead it into a neat ball. Flatten it into a disc, cover and chill for at least 1 hour.

3. Make the filling. While the dough is chilling, in a large mixing bowl, whisk the lemon zest and juice, passion-fruit pulp and caster sugar with a balloon whisk until combined and the sugar dissolves. Whisk in the eggs and salt until combined, then add the cream and whisk again until smooth. Strain the mixture through a sieve into a large jug, cover and chill until ready to use.

4. Blind bake the tart case. Roll out the pastry on a lightly floured work surface into a neat round, about 32cm in diameter and 3mm thick. Line the tin with the pastry, pressing it into the bottom and grooves. Trim and discard the excess and chill for 20 minutes.

5. Heat the oven to 180°C/160°C fan/Gas 4, placing a baking sheet on the middle shelf of the oven to heat up at the same time.

6. Prick the base of the pastry case with a fork, then line it with baking paper and fill it with baking beans or rice. Place the tin on the hot baking sheet and bake for 20 minutes, until the edges start to turn crisp and golden. Remove the paper and beans or rice and bake for a further 5 minutes to cook the base.

7. Brush the beaten egg white over the base of the pastry in a thin layer and return it to the oven for 2 minutes – the egg white forms a seal between the pastry and the filling, stopping the pastry case from becoming soggy.

Continues overleaf

8. Turn the oven down to 130°C/110°C fan/Gas 1.

9. Assemble and bake the tart. Place the cooked pastry case (still on the baking sheet) on the middle shelf of the oven and carefully pour in the lemon and passion-fruit filling. Bake for 45 minutes, until the filling is just set but with a slight wobble. Remove the tart from the oven and leave it to cool, then chill until you're ready to serve.

10. Finish the tart. Remove the tart from the tin and place it on a serving plate. Dust the top with an even layer of icing sugar and, using a kitchen blowtorch, caramelise it. Leave the topping for 5 minutes for the sugar to harden and crisp, then serve the tart with a spoonful (a quenelle looks pretty) of crème fraîche, and extra passion-fruit pulp spooned over the top, if you wish.

Makes 24
Hands on 2 hours
+ macerating
Bake 20 mins

For the mincemeat
1 Bramley apple, peeled,
    cored and diced
100g raisins
100g sultanas
100g dried cranberries
60g glacé cherries, quartered
60g dried apricots, chopped
60g dried pitted dates,
    chopped
60g mixed peel
60g blanched almonds,
    chopped
20g crystallised ginger,
    chopped
finely grated zest and
    juice of 1 orange
finely grated zest and juice
    of 1 unwaxed lemon
finely grated zest and juice
    of 1 unwaxed lime
150g light muscovado sugar
2 tsp rosewater
2 tsp angostura bitters
2 tsp vanilla paste
1 tsp mixed spice
1 tsp ground cinnamon
1 tsp ground nutmeg
½ tsp ground cloves
½ tsp salt
90g unsalted butter, diced
50ml brandy
40ml amaretto

Continues overleaf

Mince pies

*Christmas begins when I make my mincemeat – the smell alone is festive
and fills me with comfort and joy. My favourite way to spread the festive
cheer is making mince pies and gifting them in little packages. I've never
been a particular fan of mince pies myself, but everyone else loves them!*

1. Make the mincemeat filling. Mix together the apple, all the dried
fruits, mixed peel, almonds, ginger and citrus zests in a large mixing
bowl. Add the muscovado sugar, pour over the citrus juices, rosewater,
angostura bitters and vanilla. Add the spices and salt and mix again
until thoroughly incorporated. Cover and chill for at least 2 hours,
but ideally overnight (or up to 1 week), occasionally stirring and
re-covering, to macerate the fruit.

2. Transfer the fruit mixture to a saucepan and add the butter. Heat
on a medium–low heat until the butter melts, gently stirring to combine.
Continue to cook gently for 10 minutes, until the fruit is plump, the
apple softens, and the juices thicken, stirring occasionally to prevent
the mixture catching on the bottom of the pan. Tip the mincemeat into
a bowl and leave to cool. Stir the brandy and amaretto into the cooled
mincemeat until combined. Cover until ready to use.

3. Make the pastry. Using your fingertips, rub the butter into the flour
in a mixing bowl until the mixture resembles breadcrumbs. Mix in the
icing sugar and grated citrus zests until combined. Add the yolks and
vanilla, the pinch of salt and 1 tablespoon of cold water. Mix first using
a table knife and then your hands until the mixture starts to come
together into a dough, adding a little more water, if needed. Give the
dough a quick knead with your hands to bring it together into a ball.
Flatten it into a disc, cover and chill for 1 hour while you make the
topping and filling.

4. Make the marzipan. Combine the ground almonds and sugar in
a mixing bowl. Add the glucose, almond extract and amaretto and mix
to a lumpy dough. Tip the dough onto the work surface and knead until
it comes together into a ball. Cover and freeze until ready to use.

5. Make the frangipane filling. Beat the butter in a stand mixer
fitted with the beater, on medium speed for about 2 minutes, or by
hand, until light and creamy. Beat in the caster sugar until pale and
fluffy. Gradually add the eggs, beating well between each addition.
Mix in both types of almond and the flour and set aside.

Continues overleaf

Dessert

Mince pies (continued)

For the shortcrust pastry
250g unsalted butter,
    diced and chilled
450g plain flour
75g icing sugar, sifted
finely grated zest of ½ orange
finely grated zest of
    1 unwaxed lemon
finely grated zest of
    1 unwaxed lime
2 large egg yolks
1 tsp vanilla paste
pinch of salt

For the marzipan topping
100g ground almonds
50g icing sugar, sifted
1 tsp liquid glucose
½ tsp almond extract
20ml amaretto

For the frangipane filling
100g unsalted butter
100g caster sugar
2 large eggs, lightly beaten
100g ground almonds
50g chopped blanched
    almonds
70g plain flour

YOU WILL NEED
10cm round, fluted
    cookie cutter
12-hole muffin tins
    x 2, greased

6. Heat the oven to 200°C/180°C fan/Gas 6 with 2 baking sheets inside.

7. Assemble the mince pies. Roll out the pastry on a lightly floured work surface until about 2mm thick. Stamp out 24 discs using the fluted cookie cutter, re-rolling the pastry if needed, and use these to line the muffin tins.

8. Spoon 1 tablespoon of the mincemeat into each muffin cup. Any remaining mincemeat will store well in a sealed, sterilised jar or in a lidded plastic food box in the fridge for up to 2 months.

9. Spread a heaped teaspoon of frangipane on top of the mincemeat, just enough to almost fill the pastry case without it overflowing.

10. Coarsely grate a small amount of frozen marzipan onto the top of the frangipane filling in each mince pie.

11. Bake the mince pies for 15–20 minutes on the hot baking sheets until golden brown. To check the bottom of the mince pies are baked, remove one of them from the tins – it should be lightly browned and crisp. Otherwise, return the tins to the oven for a few more minutes.

12. As soon as the pies come out of the oven, carefully transfer them to a wire rack to cool, so they don't stick in the tins. Dust with icing sugar before serving. They are especially good with some brandy butter.

Serves 8
Hands on 1 hour + chilling
Bake 1 hour

For the syrup
125g runny honey
40g caster sugar
1 cinnamon stick
juice of ½ lemon
2 strips of orange peel
1 tsp rosewater

For the nut layer
75g blanched almonds
75g unsalted pistachios
50g walnuts
25g sesame seeds
1 tsp ground cinnamon
½ tsp ground cardamom
1 tsp finely grated orange zest

For the cheesecake
550g cream cheese
150g soured cream
150g Greek-style yoghurt
100g caster sugar
2 tsp cornflour
1 tsp vanilla paste
3 eggs, lightly beaten
50g unsalted butter, melted
200g filo pastry

To decorate
seeds from ½ pomegranate
edible dried rose petals
    (optional)

YOU WILL NEED
20cm springform tin,
    base-lined with
    baking paper

Baklava cheesecake

Cheesecake and Mediterranean holidays all wrapped into one. There is a gorgeous combination of sweet–sour flavours and of creamy–crunchy textures in this aromatic dessert.

1. Make the syrup. In a small pan, bring the honey, sugar, cinnamon stick, lemon juice, orange peel and 75ml of water to the boil over a medium heat. Stir to dissolve the sugar, then reduce the heat slightly and simmer for 6–7 minutes, until the syrup reduces by one-third. Remove the pan from the heat, add the rosewater and leave to cool.

2. Heat the oven to 170°C/150°C fan/Gas 3.

3. Make the nut layer. Pulse the almonds, pistachios and walnuts in a food processor until chopped to a fine rubble. Tip the mixture onto a baking tray and toast it in the oven for 6 minutes, until starting to turn golden. Add the sesame seeds and toast for a further 2 minutes. Tip the mixture into a bowl, add the cinnamon, cardamom, orange zest and 2 tablespoons of the honey syrup and mix to combine.

4. Make the cheesecake. Using a rubber spatula or wooden spoon, beat the cream cheese, 100g of the soured cream, 100g of the yoghurt, and all of the caster sugar and the cornflour in a mixing bowl until smooth and thoroughly combined. Add 2 tablespoons of the honey syrup and the vanilla and mix again until smooth. Beat in the eggs until thoroughly combined. Set aside.

5. Assemble the cheesecake. Liberally brush the inside of the lined cake tin with a little of the melted butter. Brush one sheet of filo with melted butter and lay it centrally in the tin covering the base and coming up the sides, leaving the excess overhanging.

6. Brush the next filo sheet with butter and place in the tin, again covering the base but at a slight angle to the first sheet of filo. Gently press the filo layers together into the base being careful not to rip the delicate sheets.

7. Repeat with a further 2 sheets of filo – the base and sides of the tin should now be evenly lined with 4 layers of filo. Spoon two-thirds of the nut mixture into the tin and press to cover the base in an even layer. Brush another sheet of filo with butter and lay it in the tin on top of the nuts, overhanging the sides as before. Reserve the remaining nut mixture.

Continues overleaf

8. Place the tin on a baking tray and pour in the cheesecake mixture. Using scissors, snip the overhanging filo from the edges of the tin leaving an edge of 2–3cm. Bake for 40–45 minutes, until just set but with a slight wobble in the middle.

9. Meanwhile, mix the remaining soured cream and yoghurt with 1 tablespoon of the honey syrup. Carefully spoon this on top of the cheesecake and return it to the oven for a further 10 minutes, until the filling sets and the filo pastry is golden brown. Leave to cool to room temperature, then chill for 3–4 hours or overnight, until set and you are ready to serve.

10. Unclip the sides of the tin and carefully release the cheesecake. If the pastry on the sides of the cheesecake has not crisped, put it into an oven heated to 180°C/160°C fan/Gas 4 for 5 minutes. Chill again for 30 minutes before serving.

11. Scatter the remaining nut mixture, along with the pomegranate seeds and rose petals, if using, on top of the cheesecake and drizzle with honey syrup to serve.

Serves 12
Hands on 1 hour + chilling
Bake 35 mins

For the pastry
250g plain flour
pinch of salt
125g unsalted butter,
    chilled and cubed
2–3 tbsp ice-cold water

For the caramel
200g caster sugar
200g double cream
225g unsalted butter, cubed
2 tsp vanilla extract
½ tsp crushed sea salt

For the topping
2 large ripe bananas,
    cut into 1cm thick slices
300ml double cream
1 tsp vanilla extract
15g icing sugar, sifted
10g 70% dark chocolate,
    very finely grated

YOU WILL NEED
 23cm straight-sided,
    loose-bottomed tart tin
baking beans or rice
sugar thermometer
cake-decorating turntable
large piping bag fitted with
    a large ribbon nozzle

Paul's banoffee pie

*The original banoffee pie, a British dessert developed in the 1970s, has
a pastry crust, rather than a biscuit base. And that's exactly how Paul
wanted this one – a nostalgic recreation of an original banoffee pie,
with a beautiful finish that makes it fit for an elegant party dessert.*

1. Make the pastry. Tip the flour and salt into a mixing bowl. Add
the chilled, diced butter and cut the butter into the flour using a
round-bladed knife or palette knife. Using your hands, rub the butter
into the flour until there are only very small flecks still visible.

2. Make a well in the centre of the mixture, add the ice-cold water
and, using the knife, cut the wet ingredients into the dry, then gather
the pastry into a ball. Flatten the pastry into a disc, cover and chill
for 30 minutes, until firm.

3. Roll out the pastry on a lightly floured work surface to a neat disc,
about 2–3mm thick and large enough to line the base and sides of the
tin. Carefully line the tin, then trim any excess from the top and prick
the base with a fork. Chill for 30 minutes.

4. Heat the oven to 190°C/170°C fan/Gas 5. Line the pastry case with
baking paper and baking beans or rice, and place it on a solid baking
sheet. Bake for about 25 minutes, until the edges are golden. Remove
the paper and beans or rice and bake for a further 10 minutes to dry
out the base. Leave the pastry case to cool.

5. Make the caramel. Heat the caster sugar in a saucepan over a
medium heat, swirling the pan from time to time, until the sugar dissolves
and turns an amber colour. While the caramel is cooking, bring the cream
to a simmer in a separate pan over a medium heat, then immediately
remove it from the heat and set aside.

6. Once the caramel is amber-coloured, carefully pour in the warm
cream (be careful as it will splutter) and stir to combine. Add the butter,
stirring continuously, until it forms a smooth caramel. Increase the heat
to high and boil until the mixture reaches 106°C on a sugar thermometer.

7. Immediately remove the pan from the heat. Stir in the vanilla and
salt, then pour the caramel into a heatproof jug (to halt the cooking
process) and leave to cool until just warm.

Continues overleaf

8. Pour the caramel into the baked pastry case and place it in the fridge for 2 hours, until set.

9. Make the topping. Arrange the banana slices over the set caramel, sitting them snugly together to make an even layer. Place the tart on the cake-decorating turntable.

10. Lightly whip the cream with the vanilla and icing sugar until it just holds its shape. Spoon the cream into the piping bag fitted with the large ribbon nozzle.

11. Starting from the outside edge, pipe 5cm-diameter semi-circular petals around the edge of the pastry. Continue piping petals in concentric circles until you reach the middle of the pie. The top should look like a large flower head.

12. Finish the top of the pie with a sprinkling of very finely grated chocolate, to help define the petals.

50g sultanas
50g raisins
25g mixed candied peel
finely grated zest of
    ½ unwaxed lemon
finely grated zest of ½ orange
75ml marsala
1 tsp ground cinnamon
1 tsp mixed spice
300ml whole milk
300ml double cream,
    plus extra to serve
½ vanilla pod, split lengthways
500g panettone or pandoro,
    sliced horizontally into
    2cm-thick discs, then
    each slice quartered
50g unsalted butter,
    very softened, plus
    extra for greasing
100g marzipan,
    cut into 5mm dice
4 eggs
100g caster sugar
pinch of salt
freshly grated nutmeg
2 tbsp demerara sugar
just-boiled water,
    from a kettle

YOU WILL NEED
30 x 20cm ovenproof
    dish, greased

panettone bread and butter pudding

Wholesome bread-and-butter pudding is given the Christmas treatment in this Anglo-Italian fusion dessert. It's warming, it's boozy and it's divine. And, of course, it's not just for Christmas – use brioche and a little extra dried fruit if you can't find panettone.

1. Soak the dried fruit. Combine the sultanas, raisins and candied peel in a small bowl. Add the lemon and orange zests, marsala, cinnamon and mixed spice and mix well to combine. Cover and leave to steep overnight for the fruit to absorb the marsala or, if you're in a hurry, heat the mixture in the microwave for 30 seconds and leave for 2 hours to soak.

2. Heat the milk, cream and split vanilla pod in a pan to just below boiling. Remove from the heat and leave to infuse for 30 minutes.

3. Heat the oven to 180°C/160°C fan/Gas 4.

4. Scatter one-third of the soaked dried fruit into the bottom of the greased ovenproof dish.

5. Lightly spread each piece of panettone with the softened butter, then arrange the slices in the dish, scattering the marzipan and more dried fruit between each layer.

6. Whisk the eggs with the caster sugar and salt with a balloon whisk in a large mixing bowl. Strain in the vanilla-infused milk mixture and give it a whisk to combine.

7. Assemble the pudding. Ladle the custard mixture over the bread slices until almost covered, then finely grate a little nutmeg over the top and scatter with the demerara sugar. Place the dish in a large roasting tin and pour in enough just-boiled water to come halfway up the sides of the dish.

8. Bake the pudding. Carefully slide the pudding dish into the oven and bake for about 30 minutes, until the custard is just set with a good wobble in the middle and the top of the pudding is golden and crisp. Leave the pudding to sit for 3–4 minutes, then serve with extra cream poured over.

Serves 8–10
Hands on 1½ hours
+ cooling and chilling
Bake 50 mins

For the biscuit base
250g plain flour
60g wholewheat flour
100g dark brown soft sugar
1 tsp baking powder
½ tsp bicarbonate of soda
½ tsp salt
¼ tsp ground cinnamon
210g unsalted butter,
    chilled and diced
2 balls of stem ginger,
    finely chopped
85g runny honey
60g whole milk
1 tsp vanilla extract

For the filling
6–8 unwaxed limes
200g double cream
5 egg yolks
1 x 397g tin of condensed milk

For the Chantilly topping
200g double cream
20g icing sugar, sifted
½ tsp vanilla extract

To decorate
2 limes, halved
    and finely sliced

YOU WILL NEED
2 baking sheets, each
    lined with baking paper
    or a silicone mat
20cm springform tin,
    greased, then based-lined
    with baking paper
medium piping bag fitted
    with a medium ribbon
    nozzle (optional)

Key lime pie

I make this pie for special occasions, including every year for my wife's get together with her teacher friends at Christmas. It looks impressive, but it's easy to put together and has that home-spun American feel.

1. Make the biscuit base. In a large mixing bowl, mix together both flours, and the dark brown sugar, baking powder, bicarbonate of soda, salt and ground cinnamon. Add 115g of the butter and the stem ginger and rub in the butter with your fingertips until the mixture resembles breadcrumbs.

2. In a separate bowl, mix the honey, milk and vanilla, then mix this into the dry ingredients to form a smooth dough. Cover and chill for 1 hour, until firm. Heat the oven to 180°C/160°C fan/Gas 4.

3. Roll out the dough on a lightly floured work surface until about 3mm thick. Cut the dough into 6cm squares and place these on the lined baking sheets. Prick with a fork and bake for 15–16 minutes, until golden brown around the edges and firm. Transfer to a wire rack to cool.

4. Weigh out 350g of the biscuits and blitz them in a food processor to fine crumbs. Tip the crumbs into a large mixing bowl. Melt the remaining 95g of butter, then pour it over the biscuit crumbs and mix to combine. Tip the buttery crumbs into the lined springform tin and, using a measuring cup, or equivalent, carefully press the crumbs into the base and up the sides into a firm, even layer. Place the tin on a baking sheet and bake for 8–10 minutes, until crisp and golden. Leave to cool.

5. Reheat the oven to 160°C/140°C fan/Gas 2–3.

6. Make the filling. Finely grate the zest of 4 limes and squeeze the juice of 6–8 (you need 150ml). Mix the zest and juice with the double cream in a large mixing bowl. Add the yolks, whisk to combine, then add the condensed milk and whisk until smooth. Pour into the biscuit case, then bake the pie for 20–25 minutes, until just set. Cool, then chill overnight.

7. Make the Chantilly topping. Whisk the cream, icing sugar and vanilla in a stand mixer fitted with the whisk on a low speed until the mixture thickens into ribbons – don't overmix; it may be a good idea to start in the stand mixer, then finish by hand to ensure the right consistency.

8. Assemble the pie. Spoon the Chantilly cream into the medium piping bag fitted with the ribbon nozzle and pipe the cream around the edge of the pie (or spoon the cream over the top of the pie to cover). Decorate with slices of lime.

Makes 6
Hands on 1 hour + cooling
Bake 17 mins

For the caramel
75g light muscovado sugar
50g golden syrup
50g unsalted butter
125ml double cream,
   plus extra to serve
75g caster sugar
pinch of sea-salt flakes
1 tsp vanilla paste

For the puddings
30g 70% dark chocolate,
   broken into pieces
175g unsalted butter,
   at room temperature
100g light muscovado sugar
50g caster sugar
2 eggs, lightly beaten
1 egg yolk
1 tsp vanilla paste
125g plain flour
½ tsp baking powder
pinch of salt
vanilla ice cream or double
   cream, to serve (optional)

YOU WILL NEED
sugar thermometer
6 individual (175ml) pudding
   basins, greased with butter
   and dusted with flour

Salted caramel self-saucing puddings

Brilliant for making in advance for a stress-free dinner party, or for reheating when you need ready-to-go indulgence on the sofa, these are individual pots of joy. Store any leftover caramel in the fridge in an airtight container for up to two weeks and use it over ice cream.

1. Make the caramel. Warm the muscovado sugar, syrup, butter and cream in a small saucepan over a low heat until the butter melts and the sugar dissolves. Stir until smooth. When hot, take the pan off the heat.

2. Place the caster sugar in a small pan with 1 tablespoon of water and set over a low heat to dissolve the sugar. Swirl the pan to ensure that the sugar dissolves evenly (don't stir). Use a pastry brush dipped in hot water to dissolve any crystals that form on the inside of the pan. Bring to the boil, then simmer to an amber caramel, swirling the pan occasionally.

3. Slide the pan off the heat and pour the hot cream mixture into the caramel. Stir until smooth, then simmer over a medium heat for a further 3 minutes, until the caramel reaches 118°C on the sugar thermometer. Slide the pan off the heat and stir in the salt flakes and vanilla. Pour the hot caramel into a bowl and leave to cool for at least 2 hours.

4. Make the puddings. Melt the chocolate in short bursts in a microwave (or in a bain marie) and set aside. Beat the butter and both sugars in a stand mixer fitted with the beater, on medium speed for 3–5 minutes, until pale and creamy, scraping down the inside of the bowl as necessary. Gradually add the eggs, beating well between each addition. Add the egg yolk and vanilla and combine. Mix in the melted chocolate, then sift in the flour, baking powder and salt and mix on a low speed until combined.

5. Spoon the mixture into the prepared pudding basins until each is half full. Heat a teaspoon in a cup of hot water and press it into the mixture to make an indent. Spoon a rounded teaspoonful of the cold caramel into the indent and cover with the remaining pudding mixture. Cover and chill the puddings for 2–4 hours.

6. Heat the oven to 180°C/160°C fan/Gas 4.

7. Place the pudding basins on a baking tray and bake for 15–17 minutes, until well-risen and golden brown. Working quickly turn out the puddings onto plates and serve with more of the caramel, warmed, and with double cream or vanilla ice cream.

Serves 8
Hands on 1 hour + chilling
Bake 1 hour 10 mins

For the pastry
250g plain flour, plus
    extra for rolling out
pinch of salt
150g unsalted butter,
    cubed and chilled
50g icing sugar, sifted
1 egg, separated
2–3 tbsp ice-cold water
1 tsp lemon juice

For the filling
3 Bramley apples
2 small Braeburn
    or Cox apples
300g blackberries
3 tbsp golden caster
    sugar, plus extra
    for sprinkling
juice of ½ lemon
1 tbsp cornflour
1 tsp ground cinnamon

For the crumble
100g plain flour
75g unsalted butter,
    cubed and chilled
50g golden caster sugar
pinch of salt

YOU WILL NEED
heavy pie tin (20cm
    diameter at the base)

Apple and blackberry crumble pie

When you can't decide on apple pie or crumble for a pudding after a hearty Sunday roast, this gem of a dessert saves you the agony of making a decision. Serve it with custard, cream or ice cream – or all three.

1. Make the pastry. Tip the flour, salt and butter into a large bowl and rub the butter into the flour until only small pieces of butter remain. Add the icing sugar and mix to combine. Make a well in the centre, add the egg yolk, ice-cold water and lemon juice and mix with a palette or table knife, then use your hands to bring the dough together.

2. Tip out the dough onto your work surface, knead it very briefly and shape it into a ball. Flatten the ball into a disc, cover and chill it for 1 hour until firm.

3. Roll out the dough on a lightly floured work surface into a neat, 28cm disc, about 3–4mm thick. Line the pie tin with the pastry, pressing it into the corners. Trim any excess and crimp the top pastry edge between your fingers. Chill for at about 30 minutes.

4. While the pastry is chilling, heat the oven to 190°C/170°C fan/Gas 5.

5. Prepare the filling. Peel, core and thinly slice all the apples and tip them into a large mixing bowl. Add the blackberries, caster sugar, lemon juice, cornflour and cinnamon and mix to combine. Set aside.

6. Prepare the crumble. Combine all the crumble ingredients in a bowl and, using your fingers, rub the butter into the flour until the mixture resembles breadcrumbs.

7. Assemble and bake the pie. Scoop the fruit mixture and any juices into the chilled pastry-lined pie tin and scatter with the crumble mixture. Brush the edges of the pastry with lightly beaten egg white and sprinkle over the top with a little golden caster sugar.

8. Bake the pie for 15 minutes, then lower the oven temperature to 180°C/160°C fan/Gas 4 and bake for a further 50–55 minutes, until the pastry and crumble are golden and the filling is bubbling and tender.

9. Leave the pie to rest in the tin for 5 minutes, then serve it in slices with custard, cream or ice cream.

Chocolate

Serves 10
Hands on 2 hours + cooling
Bake 30 mins

For the sponges
125g unsalted butter, softened
250g caster sugar
75g sunflower or other
    flavourless oil
4 eggs, lightly beaten
1 tsp vanilla paste
250g plain flour
30g cocoa powder
25g malted milk powder
2 tsp baking powder
½ tsp bicarbonate of soda
pinch of salt
4 tbsp whole milk
4 tbsp soured cream

For the honeycomb
1 tsp bicarbonate of soda
200g caster sugar
75g golden syrup
pinch of salt
75g milk chocolate, chopped

For the buttercream
175g 70% dark chocolate,
    chopped
150g unsalted butter, diced
400g icing sugar, sifted
40g malted milk powder
10g cocoa powder
175g soured cream
pinch of salt

For the caramel drip
50g golden syrup
50g unsalted butter
100ml double cream
100g caster sugar
pinch of sea-salt flakes
1 tsp vanilla paste

YOU WILL NEED
18cm round cake tins x 2,
    greased, then lined (base
    and sides) with baking paper
sugar thermometer
small roasting tin (at least 4cm
    deep), greased with oil and
    lined (base and sides) with
    baking paper
medium piping bag fitted with
    a medium open star nozzle
small piping bag

Malted chocolate and honeycomb layer cake

This cake – layers of chocolate sponge and fudgy buttercream – is a chocolate-lover's dream, topped off with a golden crown of milk-chocolate drizzled honeycomb. You'll have honeycomb left over – for nibbling!

1. Heat the oven to 180°C/160°C fan/Gas 4.

2. Make the sponges. Beat the butter and caster sugar in a stand mixer fitted with the beater, on medium speed for 2 minutes, until pale and creamy. Reduce the speed to low and add the sunflower (or other) oil. Scrape down the inside of the bowl and then continue to beat for a further 3 minutes, until the mixture is very pale and fluffy. Gradually add the eggs, scraping down the inside of the bowl from time to time. Add the vanilla and mix again.

3. Sift in the flour, cocoa, malted milk powder, baking powder, bicarbonate of soda and salt. Using a spatula, fold in the dry ingredients until almost combined, then add the milk and soured cream and beat for 30 seconds on a low speed until smooth. Divide the mixture equally between the lined tins and spread it level with a palette knife. Bake on the middle shelf for 25–30 minutes, until well-risen, golden brown and a skewer inserted into the centre of each sponge comes out clean. Leave to cool in the tins for 5 minutes, then turn out onto a wire rack to cool completely.

4. Make the honeycomb. While the cakes are cooling, sift the bicarbonate of soda into a small bowl and have a whisk and rubber spatula to hand.

5. Add the sugar, golden syrup, salt and 75ml of water to a medium pan and place over a medium–low heat to dissolve the sugar, stirring occasionally. Once the sugar has dissolved, place a sugar thermometer into the pan and bring the mixture to the boil. Continue to cook at a gentle boil until the mixture reaches 150°C. Working quickly, remove the pan from the heat and whisk in the sifted bicarbonate of soda for about 5 seconds, until thoroughly combined – take care as the caramel will foam ferociously. Using a rubber spatula, scoop the mixture into the prepared roasting tin in an even layer but do not spread it out as you don't want to deflate the honeycomb. Leave for 2–3 hours to cool and harden.

6. Make the buttercream frosting. While the honeycomb is cooling, melt the dark chocolate and butter in a heatproof bowl set over a pan of barely simmering water, and stir until smooth. Remove the bowl from the heat and leave the chocolate to cool for 5 minutes.

Continues overleaf

7. Sift the icing sugar, malted milk powder and cocoa into a large mixing bowl. Add the soured cream and salt and whisk until thoroughly combined. Add the chocolate mixture and whisk again until the frosting is smooth and thick enough to spread. Scoop 3–4 tablespoons of the buttercream into the medium piping bag fitted with the open star nozzle and set aside to decorate later. Cover the remainder and set aside.

8. Make the caramel drip. Warm the golden syrup, butter and cream in a saucepan over a gentle heat to melt the butter. Stir until smooth and set aside. Place the caster sugar in a small saucepan with 1 tablespoon of water over a low heat. Swirl (but don't stir) to dissolve the sugar. Bring to the boil and cook for about 2 minutes to an amber-coloured caramel. Remove from the heat and add the hot cream mixture. Stir, then return the pan to a medium heat and simmer for 3 minutes until thick enough to coat the back of a spoon. Remove from the heat, add the sea-salt flakes and vanilla and stir to combine. Leave until cold and then scoop into the small piping bag. Snip the end into a 3mm point.

9. Assemble the cake. Trim the domed top off each sponge and cut each in half horizontally to make 4 cake layers. Place 1 sponge on a serving plate and spread 3 heaped tablespoons of the frosting from the bowl over the top. Place a second sponge on top. Repeat with the frosting and sponges, ending with the fourth sponge. Lightly press, then chill for 15 minutes.

10. Evenly cover the top and sides of the cake with the remaining frosting in the bowl. Leave to set for 20 minutes at room temperature.

11. Meanwhile, melt the milk chocolate in a heatproof bowl set over a pan of barely simmering water and stir until smooth. Remove the bowl from the heat and leave the chocolate to cool for 3–4 minutes.

12. Turn the honeycomb out of the tin, then break it into bite-sized chunks on a sheet of baking paper. Drizzle the melted milk chocolate over the honeycomb and leave it to set and harden for about 20 minutes.

13. Pipe the caramel drip all around the top edge of the cake, letting it run down the sides.

14. Arrange the honeycomb pieces around the top edge, then crush some of the remaining honeycomb into smaller pieces and press these around the bottom edge to create a skirt. Finally, use the frosting in the piping bag to pipe kisses over the top of the cake to finish.

Makes 12
Hands on 1 hour
Bake 20 mins

For the cakes
120g blanched hazelnuts
115g unsalted butter
100g plain flour
20g cocoa powder
½ tsp baking powder
½ tsp bicarbonate of soda
pinch of salt
100g golden caster sugar
100g light brown soft sugar
125g soured cream or
   buttermilk, at room
   temperature
2 eggs, lightly beaten
1 tsp vanilla paste

For the praline
25g caster sugar
pinch of salt

For the ganache glaze
125ml double cream
50ml whole milk
30g golden syrup
150g 70% dark chocolate,
   finely chopped
pinch of salt

YOU WILL NEED
12-hole muffin tin, greased,
   then holes base-lined
   with baking paper
plate lined with baking paper
small piping bag fitted
   with a medium closed star
   nozzle

Chocolate and hazelnut mini cakes

These fancy little cakes might remind you of a certain chocolate to indulge in at a glitzy party for foreign dignitaries! Make the cakes a day ahead as they keep well and the nutty chocolate flavour improves with time.

1. Heat the oven to 180°C/160°C fan/Gas 4.

2. Make the cakes. Tip the hazelnuts into a small roasting tin and toast in the oven for about 5 minutes, until golden brown. Leave to cool, then blitz 75g of the nuts in a food processor until very finely chopped. Set aside the remainder.

3. Melt the butter in a small saucepan over a medium–low heat and cook, swirling the pan occasionally, until the butter foams and the milk solids turn golden brown. Pour the browned butter and speckles into a bowl and leave to cool for 5 minutes.

4. Sift the flour, cocoa, baking powder, bicarbonate of soda and salt into a mixing bowl. Add both sugars and the finely chopped hazelnuts and mix with a balloon whisk until combined. Make a well in the centre of the dry ingredients and add the brown butter, soured cream or buttermilk, eggs and vanilla and whisk to thoroughly combine.

5. Divide the mixture equally between the holes in the muffin tin and spread level. Bake for 18–20 minutes, until well risen, golden brown, and a skewer inserted into the centre of one of the sponges comes out clean. Leave the sponges to cool in the tin for 2 minutes, then turn them out onto a wire rack to cool completely.

6. Make the praline. Gently heat the sugar with 2 teaspoons of water in a small saucepan over a low heat, without stirring, until it dissolves. Increase the heat, bring the sugar to the boil and continue to cook, swirling the pan occasionally (but don't stir), until the syrup becomes an amber-coloured caramel.

7. Set aside 12 of the remaining hazelnuts to decorate. Stir the rest with the salt into the caramel until coated.

Continues overleaf

8. Tip the mixture onto the plate lined with baking paper and leave to cool and harden. When cool, break the praline into smaller pieces, then blitz in a mini food processor until very finely chopped and almost smooth.

9. Make the ganache glaze. Heat the cream, milk and syrup in a small saucepan until steaming hot but not boiling. Tip the dark chocolate into a medium mixing bowl, add the hot cream mixture and leave for 1 minute, then stir until silky smooth. Stir in the salt and leave to cool for 5 minutes. Spoon 75g of the ganache into a bowl and set aside to decorate.

10. Place the cakes upside down on a wire rack over a sheet of baking, paper to catch any drips, and carefully spoon over the ganache glaze and gently spread it over the cakes with a palette knife. Leave to set at room temperature.

11. Using a balloon whisk, whisk the reserved 75g of ganache until thickened. Mix in the praline and scoop the mixture into the piping bag fitted with the medium star nozzle. Pipe a swirl of praline ganache on top of the cakes and decorate each with one of the reserved hazelnuts.

Serves 4–6
Hands on 20 mins
Bake 25 mins

For the cake
100g 70% dark chocolate,
    chopped
125g unsalted butter, diced
150ml freshly boiled water
100g caster sugar
75g light brown soft sugar
2 eggs
1 tsp vanilla extract
125g plain flour
15g cocoa powder
½ tsp baking powder
½ tsp bicarbonate of soda
pinch of salt
50g pecans, chopped

For the chocolate sauce
150g 70% dark chocolate,
    chopped
100g light brown soft sugar
300ml double cream
50g unsalted butter, diced
1 tsp vanilla extract
pinch of salt

YOU WILL NEED
ovenproof skillet
    (18–20cm-diameter base;
    4–5cm deep), greased

Chocolate skillet cake

*On the table in under an hour, this is one to serve in the pan with
ice-cream melting on top. Give everyone a spoon to tuck in. Need
we say more?*

1. Heat the oven to 180°C/160°C fan/Gas 4.

2. Make the cake. Combine the chocolate, butter and 75ml of the
freshly boiled water in a small, heatproof bowl and place the bowl
over a pan of barely simmering water. Stir until the chocolate and
butter have melted and the mixture is smooth.

3. Tip both sugars into a large mixing bowl. Add the eggs and vanilla
and use a balloon whisk to beat for about 2 minutes, until paler and
thoroughly combined.

4. Add the melted chocolate mixture and stir to just combine. Sift
the flour, cocoa, baking powder, bicarbonate of soda and a pinch
of salt into the bowl and mix again until smooth. Add the remaining
75ml of freshly boiled water and beat to combine.

5. Scoop the mixture into the greased skillet, spread it level and bake
for 22–25 minutes, until risen and the cake mixture is just cooked.

6. Make the chocolate sauce. While the cake is baking, combine all
the sauce ingredients in a small saucepan. Add 5 tablespoons of water
and place the pan over a low heat. Stir regularly until the chocolate
and butter have melted and the sauce is smooth, but don't let the
sauce boil.

7. Finish the cake. When the cake is ready, immediately spoon
4 tablespoons of the chocolate sauce over the top, scatter with
the pecans and return the skillet to the oven for 1–2 minutes,
until the sauce bubbles at the edges of the cake.

8. Leave to cool for 2 minutes, then serve with the remaining sauce,
and with scoops of vanilla ice cream gently melting on the top of
the cake as you all dig in.

Makes 12
Hands on 1 hour + resting,
chilling and rising
Bake 20 mins

For the dough
450g strong white bread flour,
    plus extra for rolling out
50g white rye flour
30g caster sugar
1 tbsp dried milk powder
7g fast-action dried yeast
1 tsp salt
200ml whole milk, lukewarm
3 eggs
125g unsalted butter,
    at room temperature

For the filling
finely grated zest of 1 orange
100g 54% dark chocolate,
    chopped
100g unsalted butter, diced
50g light muscovado sugar
1 tbsp cocoa powder
1 tsp vanilla paste
pinch of salt
30g pistachios, finely chopped

For the syrup
150g caster sugar
juice of 1 orange
1 cinnamon stick
2 cardamom pods, bruised

YOU WILL NEED
pizza wheel
2 baking sheets, each lined
    with baking paper
2 proving bags

Chocolate orange babka knots

*Prepare these delicious buns the night before you plan to serve them.
Then, in the morning, you simply give them a final prove and bake them
to enjoy fresh out of the oven in time for brunch. They make for a squishy,
sumptuous and well-earned pick-me-up after a bracing walk.*

1. Make the dough. Combine the flours, sugar, milk powder, yeast and salt
in the bowl of a stand mixer fitted with a dough hook. Add the warm milk
and 2 of the eggs and mix on medium–low speed until just combined.

2. Little by little, add the butter to the dough mixture. Once you've added
it all, knead the dough for 5 minutes, until it is silky smooth, elastic and
cleanly leaves the side of the mixer bowl.

3. Shape the dough into a ball, return it to the bowl, then cover and leave
at room temperature for about 1 hour or until doubled in size.

4. Prepare the filling. While the dough is rising, combine the orange zest,
chocolate, butter, sugar, cocoa and vanilla in a heatproof bowl. Add the
salt and place the bowl over a pan of barely simmering water. Heat the
mixture, stirring occasionally, until the chocolate and butter have melted
and combined. Remove the bowl from the heat and leave the filling to
cool to room temperature and thicken to a spreadable consistency.

5. Fill the dough. Turn out the risen dough onto a lightly floured work
surface. Use your hands to knock it back, then flatten it into a rectangle
and roll it out to a neat 36 x 60cm rectangle. Turn it so that you have
one of the long sides nearest to you.

6. Using an offset palette knife, spread one half of the chocolate mixture
over the right-hand third of the dough rectangle. Carefully fold this over
the middle third of dough and gently pat the two together.

7. Spread the top of this third with more chocolate spread and then fold
the left-hand third of dough over the top to cover. You should now have
a neat 36 x 20cm parcel of three layers of dough and two of filling.

8. Shape the dough. Using the pizza wheel, cut the dough horizontally
into twelve 3cm strips. Taking one strip at a time, use the pizza wheel
to cut the strip horizontally in half again, leaving 1cm uncut at the top
(fold), to keep the strip intact at one end.

Continues overleaf

9. Plait the strips together. Starting at the fold end, twist the plait into a loose knot and tuck the ends under to prevent them unravelling. Place on a lined baking sheet. Repeat with the remaining strips to make 12 buns, transferring them to the baking sheets as you go. Place each baking sheet into a proving bag, transfer them to the fridge and chill overnight.

10. The next day, leave the buns at room temperature for 1–2 hours, until the dough is puffy and springs back when gently pressed with your finger.

11. Prepare the syrup. While the dough is coming to temperature, combine the syrup ingredients in a small saucepan. Add 100ml of water and place the pan over a medium–low heat to dissolve the sugar. Bring to the boil and simmer for 2 minutes to thicken slightly.

12. Heat the oven to 190°C/170°C fan/Gas 5.

13. Bake the buns. Lightly brush the buns with the remaining beaten egg, then place them into the oven to bake for 20 minutes, until golden brown.

14. Liberally brush the warm buns with the syrup and scatter them with the chopped pistachios. Leave to cool to room temperature before serving.

Makes 16
Hands on 30 mins
Bake 35 mins

150g unsalted butter, diced
150g light brown soft sugar
50g golden caster sugar
1 tsp vanilla paste
2 eggs
150g plain flour
50g ground almonds
½ tsp baking powder
pinch of salt
175g white chocolate,
    chopped into small pieces
200g cherries, pitted
    and quartered
30g flaked almonds

YOU WILL NEED
20cm square baking tin,
    greased, then lined
    (base and sides)
    with baking paper

Cherry and almond blondies

Perfect for taking on a picnic or wrapping together as a care package, these blondies travel well and are ideal to pack into an airtight box to post to someone in need of a treat. The Bakewell flavours bring a touch of nostalgia.

1. Heat the oven to 180°C/160°C fan/Gas 4.

2. Melt the butter in a small saucepan over a medium–low heat. Continue to heat the butter, swirling the pan from time to time, for about 2 minutes, until it smells of toasted nuts and turns golden brown. Tip the brown butter into a mixing bowl and leave it to cool for 3–4 minutes.

3. Add both sugars and the vanilla to the melted butter and whisk for 1 minute with a balloon whisk to combine. Add the eggs and whisk together for 30 seconds to combine.

4. Sift the flour, ground almonds, baking powder and salt into the bowl. Add 125g of the white chocolate and all the cherries and mix with a rubber spatula until thoroughly combined. Spoon the mixture into the lined tin and spread it level with a palette knife. Scatter the flaked almonds evenly over the top.

5. Bake the blondies for 30–35 minutes, until well risen and golden brown. Leave them in the tin to cool completely.

6. Meanwhile, melt the remaining white chocolate in a heatproof bowl set over a pan of barely simmering water, or in the microwave in short bursts. Stir until smooth, then drizzle the chocolate over the cooled blondies in the tin. Leave the chocolate to set before cutting the blondies into 16 equal squares.

100g 54% dark chocolate,
chopped into 1cm chunks
225g plain flour
40g cocoa powder
1½ tsp bicarbonate of soda
pinch of salt
125g light brown soft sugar
100g caster sugar
2 eggs
200ml buttermilk
100ml sunflower oil
1 tsp vanilla extract
150g dark, milk or white
(or a mixture) chocolate
chips or chopped chocolate

YOU WILL NEED
12-hole muffin tin lined
with 12 deep paper cases

Triple chocolate muffins

These chocolate-packed muffins take moments to rustle up, making them perfect for a rainy weekend treat with tea, coffee – or hot chocolate! Of course, you should let them cool before you tuck in, but having the warm, melty chocolate drip down your chin is something else. Deep-fill paper muffin cases are best here, but regular-size will make muffins that are just as delicious – they'll just spread a little as they bake rather than rise up tall.

1. Heat the oven to 190°C/170°C fan/Gas 5.

2. Melt 50g of the dark chocolate chunks in a heatproof bowl set over a pan of barely simmering water or in the microwave in short bursts. Stir until smooth, then remove the pan from the heat, lift off the bowl and leave the chocolate to cool.

3. Meanwhile, sift the flour, cocoa, bicarbonate of soda and salt into a large mixing bowl. Mix in both sugars with a balloon whisk to combine. Make a well in the centre of the dry ingredients.

4. In a jug, lightly whisk the eggs, buttermilk, sunflower oil and vanilla, then pour the mixture into the well in the dry ingredients. Add the cooled melted chocolate and mix until just combined. Fold in two-thirds of the remaining chocolate chunks and the chocolate chips or pieces.

5. Divide the mixture equally between the muffin cases and scatter with the remaining chocolate chunks.

6. Bake the muffins for about 20 minutes, until well risen and a skewer inserted into the centres comes out with a few moist crumbs attached. Leave the muffins to cool for 5 minutes in the tin, then transfer to a wire rack to cool completely (if you can wait).

For the dacquoise
100g flaked almonds
3 egg whites (save the
    yolks for the mousse)
pinch of salt
60g caster sugar
110g icing sugar
10g cocoa powder

For the apricot and ginger compôte
200g soft dried apricots,
    roughly chopped
2 balls of stem ginger
    in syrup, drained and
    roughly chopped
25g caster sugar

For the mousse
225g 70% dark chocolate,
    chopped
50g caster sugar
1 tbsp stem ginger syrup
3 egg yolks (saved from
    the dacquoise)
250ml double cream,
    whipped to soft peaks
2 egg whites, whisked to firm
    peaks with a pinch of salt

For the glaze
125ml double cream
50g caster sugar
25g liquid glucose
200g 70% dark chocolate,
    finely chopped

To decorate
150g 70% dark chocolate,
    finely chopped
200ml double cream

YOU WILL NEED
large piping bag fitted with
    a medium plain nozzle
2 baking sheets, each lined
    with baking paper drawn
    with a 20cm-diameter circle
    (placed drawn-side down)
20cm springform tin, lined
    with a 65cm-long x
    8cm-wide acetate strip
small piping bag fitted with
    a small open star nozzle
small piping bag fitted with
    a medium ribbon nozzle

Apricot, ginger and almond chocolate mousse cake

This mousse cake is both luxurious and perfectly balanced – bitter, rich chocolate (use the best quality you can) is countered by sweet apricots and warming ginger; and the smooth mousse texture gives way to crisp almond dacquoise. Serve it to friends and enjoy the 'mmmm's.

1. Heat the oven to 180°C/160°C fan/Gas 4.

2. Make the dacquoise. Toast the flaked almonds on an unlined baking tray in the oven for about 7 minutes, until golden. Leave to cool, then whizz in a food processor until finely ground.

3. Whisk the egg whites and salt in a stand mixer fitted with the whisk on medium speed for about 2–3 minutes, until they hold soft peaks. Gradually add the caster sugar, whisking continuously until the meringue is glossy, smooth and holds firm but not dry peaks.

4. Sift the icing sugar and cocoa into the bowl, add the ground flaked almonds and fold them in using a large metal spoon or rubber spatula.

5. Scoop the mixture into the large piping bag fitted with the medium plain nozzle. Starting at the outside edge of each drawn circle on the lined baking sheets, working inwards, pipe the meringue mixture into two 20cm discs. Bake for 30 minutes, until crisp. Leave to cool.

6. Make the apricot and ginger compôte. While the dacquoise are cooling, put the apricots, stem ginger, sugar and 150ml of water in a medium saucepan. Cook over a medium–low heat, stirring to combine for about 20 minutes, until the apricots are very soft and tender and only 3 tablespoons of liquid remain in the pan. Leave to cool, then whizz in a blender or food processor until smooth. Set aside until needed.

7. Place one dacquoise layer, flat side down, in the bottom of the lined cake tin and spoon the apricot compôte on top, spreading it level with an offset palette knife. Top with the second dacquoise and gently press the layers together. Chill until needed.

8. Make the chocolate mousse. Melt the chocolate in a heatproof bowl set over a pan of barely simmering water, stir until smooth, then remove from the heat and leave to cool slightly.

9. In a small saucepan, combine the sugar and stem ginger syrup with 2 tablespoons of water and bring to the boil over a medium heat. Reduce the heat and simmer for 1 minute.

Continues overleaf

10. Tip the egg yolks into a large heatproof bowl and set over a pan of barely simmering water. Beat with an electric hand whisk to combine, then pour the hot syrup onto the egg yolks and whisk until the mixture is pale, doubled in volume, and holds a ribbon trail when you lift the whisk. Remove the bowl from the heat and whisk for 3 minutes, until cooled. Fold in the melted chocolate with a large metal spoon or rubber spatula.

11. Fold one-third of the whipped cream into the cooled chocolate mixture until almost combined. Scoop the chocolate mixture into the rest of the whipped cream and fold in until smooth.

12. Using a large metal spoon, fold one-third of the whisked egg whites into the chocolate mixture. Fold in the remaining egg whites until combined, but don't overmix. Spoon the mousse over the dacquoise, spread level, cover and chill for at least 4 hours, or overnight, until set.

13. Make the glaze. Just before the mousse cake is set, heat the cream, sugar, liquid glucose and 50ml of water in a small saucepan until steaming hot (not boiling). Tip the dark chocolate into a medium mixing bowl, add the hot cream mixture and leave for 1 minute, then stir until silky smooth. Leave to cool for 5 minutes. Spoon 3 tablespoons of the glaze into a small bowl and set aside for the decoration.

14. Remove the cake from the tin, carefully peel off the acetate strip and place the cake on a wire rack over a tray. Spoon the remaining glaze over the top and sides of the cake and use an offset palette knife to spread to a smooth, even layer. Chill for 30 minutes to firm up the glaze.

15. Make the decoration. Melt the chocolate as before. Stir until smooth. Pour the melted chocolate over the underside of a baking sheet and spread to 3mm thick. Sharply tap the baking sheet on the work surface to burst any bubbles, then chill for 15 minutes, until set but not solid.

16. Hold the blade of a kitchen knife firmly at a 45-degree angle to the chocolate and push it across the top of the chocolate to create curls. Place the curls on a baking tray and chill until ready to use.

17. Finish the cake. Place the cake on a serving plate. In a small bowl, whisk the reserved glaze until thickened to the consistency of whipped cream. Scoop into the small piping bag fitted with the small star nozzle and pipe around the bottom edge of the cake. Whip the double cream until it holds soft peaks, spoon it into the small piping bag with the medium ribbon nozzle and pipe around the top edge of the cake. Arrange the chocolate curls in the middle to decorate.

Serves 8–10
Hands on 40 mins
Bake 45 mins

For the sponge
50g 70% dark chocolate,
   broken into pieces
175g unsalted butter,
   at room temperature
50g smooth peanut butter
200g caster sugar
1 tsp vanilla paste
4 eggs, lightly beaten
4 small–medium ripe bananas
3 tbsp soured cream,
   at room temperature
225g plain flour,
   plus extra for dusting
2 tsp baking powder
1 tsp bicarbonate of soda
pinch of salt
1 tsp cocoa powder

**For the salted caramel
peanut popcorn**
2 tsp sunflower oil
25g popcorn kernels
50g caster sugar
20g unsalted butter
½ tsp vanilla paste
40g salted peanuts,
   roughly chopped

For the frosting
100g light brown soft sugar
100g dark brown soft sugar
75g unsalted butter
125ml double cream
100g 70% dark chocolate,
   chopped
large pinch of sea salt

YOU WILL NEED
2 large piping bags
2.5-litre kugelhopf/bundt tin,
   well-greased with melted
   butter and dusted with flour
baking tray lined with
   baking paper

Banana and chocolate marble cake

Do you remember how during Lockdown banana bread became every household's favourite bake? This takes that to the next level and higher – it's chocolate, banana, peanut butter, popcorn and caramel.

1. Heat the oven to 180°C/160°C fan/Gas 4 and position the shelf just below the middle of the oven.

2. Make the sponge. Melt the chocolate in a bowl set over a pan of gently simmering water, stir until smooth, and set aside.

3. Combine the butter with the peanut butter, caster sugar and vanilla in a stand mixer fitted with the beater, and beat on medium speed for 2–3 minutes, until pale. Scrape down the inside of the bowl with a spatula and gradually add the beaten eggs, mixing well between each addition.

4. In a small bowl, mash the bananas with a fork until almost smooth, add the soured cream and mix to combine.

5. Sift the flour, baking powder, bicarbonate of soda and salt into the mixer bowl. Add the mashed banana mixture and beat until smooth.

6. Spoon one third of the mixture into a clean bowl, add the melted chocolate and the cocoa powder and mix until smooth.

7. Spoon each mixture into a piping bag. Pipe a layer of banana mixture into the base of the prepared tin, followed by a layer of the chocolate mixture. Repeat, alternating the layers, until you have used up all the mixture. Tap the tin on the work surface to level and use a chopstick or skewer to very lightly marble the two mixtures together.

8. Bake for 45 minutes, until golden brown, well-risen and a skewer inserted into the centre of the sponge comes out clean. Leave the sponge to cool in the tin for 3 minutes, then turn it out onto a wire rack to cool completely.

9. Make the caramel popcorn. While the cake is cooling, heat the sunflower oil in a medium saucepan on a high heat. Add the popcorn kernels, cover with a lid and cook, shaking the pan from time to time as soon as the popping starts, until the noise stops. At this point all the kernels should have popped.

Continues overleaf

10. Tip the sugar into a small saucepan, add 2 teaspoons of water and set the pan over a medium–low heat to dissolve the sugar (don't stir).

11. Once all the sugar has dissolved, increase the heat, bring the syrup to the boil and cook without stirring until the sugar starts to turn into an amber-coloured caramel. Swirl the pan to ensure that the caramel cooks evenly. Remove the pan from the heat, add the butter and vanilla and stir to combine.

12. Quickly pour the buttery caramel over the popcorn, add the chopped peanuts and mix to combine. Tip the popcorn onto the tray lined with baking paper and leave until cold.

13. Make the frosting. Combine the sugars, butter and cream in a small saucepan over a low heat. Heat gently to dissolve the sugar and melt the butter, then increase the heat and bring the mixture to the boil. Reduce the heat again and simmer for 30 seconds. Remove the pan from the heat, add the chocolate and salt and stir until the chocolate has melted and the sauce is silky smooth. Leave to cool for 5 minutes.

14. Decorate the cake. Carefully spoon the sauce over the cold cake, leaving it to drizzle over and down the sides. Leave to set for 20 minutes, then scatter the popcorn over the top of the cake to serve.

Makes 16–25
Hands on 1 hour
+ setting and chilling
Bake 30 mins

For the shortbread
150g plain flour
15g cocoa powder
50g golden caster sugar
pinch of salt
100g unsalted butter,
    cubed and chilled
175g pecans
25g desiccated coconut

For the caramel
397g tin of condensed milk
125g unsalted butter, diced
100g golden caster sugar
2 tbsp golden syrup
1 tsp vanilla paste
pinch of sea-salt flakes

For the topping
175g 70% dark chocolate,
    broken into pieces
100g milk chocolate,
    broken into pieces
40g unsalted butter, diced
2 tbsp golden syrup
50g puffed rice
25g desiccated coconut

YOU WILL NEED
20cm square baking tin,
    lined (base and sides)
    with baking paper

Turtle bars

*These are not just turtle bars – they are turtle bars with extras.
The shortbread is, in fact, nutty chocolate shortbread. And it is topped
with nutty salted caramel before being crowned with a thick, rich, crisp
chocolate layer (itself a nod to a much-loved retro party treat). Cut them
into 25 squares, rather than 16, and squirrel away a few for yourself!*

1. Heat the oven to 180°C/160°C fan/Gas 4.

2. Make the shortbread base. Combine the flour, cocoa, sugar and salt
in a mixing bowl. Add the butter and rub it in using your fingers until the
mixture clumps together and only small flecks of butter remain. Measure
out 25g of the pecans, finely chop them, then add them to the mixture.
Add the desiccated coconut and mix with your hands to combine. Tip the
dough into the lined tin and, using your hands, press it evenly and firmly
over the base. Bake for about 25 minutes, until golden and firm.

3. Roughly chop the remaining pecans. When the shortbread base
is ready, scatter them over the top and return the tin to the oven
for a further 2 minutes. Set aside.

4. Make the caramel. While the shortbread is baking, combine the
condensed milk, butter, sugar and golden syrup in a medium, heavy-
based saucepan and set the pan over a low heat to melt the butter
and dissolve the sugar. Stirring continuously, cook over a low heat
for 10–15 minutes, until the mixture reduces, thickens enough to hold
a firm ribbon trail and turns the colour of caramel. Add the vanilla
and sea-salt flakes and mix to combine.

5. Spoon the caramel onto the shortbread over the pecans. Spread
it level and bake for 2 minutes, then leave it to cool and set it aside
for at least 4 hours, or overnight, to firm up.

6. Make the topping. Tip both chocolates into a heatproof bowl.
Add the butter and golden syrup and melt them over a pan of barely
simmering water. Stir until smooth, remove from the heat, add the
puffed rice and coconut and mix to combine.

7. Spoon the topping into the tin on top of the caramel and spread
it level. Chill for 30 minutes, until the topping has set completely.
Using a warmed knife, cut the bake into 16 (4 x 4) or 25 (5 x 5) equal
squares to serve – depending on how generous you're feeling!

Free-from

Serves 8–10
Hands on 30 mins + rising
Bake 30 mins

For the confit garlic
9 garlic cloves, peeled
100ml olive oil, plus extra
　for greasing

For the dough
300ml warm water
7g fast-action dried yeast
15g caster sugar
130g rice flour
40g tapioca flour
40g potato starch
40g cornflour
20g oat flour
15g psyllium husk powder
½ tsp xanthan gum
½ tsp fine salt
1 large egg, lightly beaten
1 tsp cider vinegar

For the topping
80g mixed pitted olives
3 rosemary sprigs, separated
　into small sprigs
sea-salt flakes

YOU WILL NEED
23cm square, shallow
　baking tin, oiled, then
　lined (base and sides)
　with baking paper

GLUTEN-FREE

Confit garlic, olive and rosemary focaccia

Squares of salty, rosemary-laced focaccia, with a saucer of olive oil for dipping, make for a much-admired nibble with drinks when your guests arrive for dinner. Garlic cloves turn sweet and silky when confited.

1. Make the confit garlic. Place the garlic cloves in a small saucepan with the oil, making sure they are fully submerged. Gently warm the oil on a very low heat for 15–20 minutes, until the garlic softens and turns light golden. Remove from the heat and strain the garlic oil through a sieve into a jug or bowl. Reserve the garlic cloves and leave the oil to cool.

2. Make the dough. While the garlic is cooking, pour the warm water into a jug. Mix in the yeast and sugar, then set the jug aside for 10 minutes, until the yeast has turned frothy.

3. Mix together the rice flour, tapioca flour, potato starch, cornflour, oat flour, psyllium husk powder, xanthan gum and salt in a stand mixer fitted with the beater, on low speed for 1 minute, until combined.

4. With the mixer still on low, add the frothy yeast liquid, along with the egg, vinegar and 4 tablespoons of the cooled garlic oil. Beat for 2 minutes, until you have a thick, sticky batter. Cover the bowl with a clean tea towel and leave the dough to rest at room temperature for 10 minutes.

5. Scrape the dough out of the bowl into the prepared tin. Oil your hands, then level the dough by patting the surface with your palms while gently pushing it towards the sides of the tin. Cover with a tea towel and leave to rise in a warm place for at least 1 hour, until doubled in size.

6. Heat the oven to 230°C/210°C fan/Gas 8.

7. Finish and bake the focaccia. Oil your fingertips and use them to press dimples into the dough. Drizzle 2 tablespoons of the remaining garlic oil over the surface of the dough, then press the olives and confit garlic into the dimples, followed by small sprigs of rosemary. Sprinkle the top of the dough with sea-salt flakes.

8. Bake the focaccia for 25–30 minutes, until risen and golden brown. Remove the focaccia from the oven and leave it to cool for 10 minutes, then remove it from the tin and place it on a wire rack to cool completely. Drizzle with the remaining garlic oil before slicing and serving.

Makes 9
Hands on 30 mins
Bake 40 mins

For the jam
100g raspberries
125g jam sugar

For the sponge
250g unsalted butter,
    softened
250g caster sugar
5 eggs
250g gluten-free
    self-raising flour
pinch of salt
100g desiccated coconut,
    plus extra to decorate
3 tbsp whole milk
custard, to serve
    (see pages 163–4)

YOU WILL NEED
sugar thermometer
23cm square cake tin,
    greased, then base-lined
    with baking paper

GLUTEN-FREE

Raspberry and coconut traybake

Jam pudding is one of those desserts that always seemed a favourite at school lunchtimes – served with spoonfuls of thick custard. This traybake is a grateful nod to those convivial childhood mealtimes – surrounded by chatter and the clanking of spoons, scraping up every last crumb.

1. Make the jam. Put the raspberries in a small saucepan, add the jam sugar and bring to the boil over a low heat. Crush the raspberries and sugar together with a potato masher, then when the sugar dissolves, increase the heat and boil for another 4 minutes, until the temperature on a sugar thermometer reaches 105°C. Remove from the heat and carefully pour the jam into a heatproof bowl. Leave to cool and set.

2. Heat the oven to 180°C/160°C fan/Gas 4.

3. Make the sponge. Beat the butter and caster sugar in a stand mixer fitted with the beater, on medium speed for 3–5 minutes, until pale and creamy, scraping down the inside of the bowl from time to time. One at a time, add the eggs, beating well between each addition.

4. Sift the flour and salt into a separate bowl and mix in the coconut. Using a rubber spatula, fold the mixture into the creamed butter mixture until just combined. Gently fold in the milk.

5. Pour the sponge mixture into the lined tin and spread it level with a palette knife. Bake on the middle shelf for about 35–40 minutes, until the sponge is well risen and golden brown, and a skewer inserted into the centre comes out clean. Leave the sponge to cool completely in the tin.

6. Decorate the traybake. Once the sponge is completely cooled, spread the jam evenly over the top, then sprinkle over the extra desiccated coconut. Cut the traybake into 9 equal squares and serve warm with custard.

Serves 16
Hands on 30 mins
+ crystallising
Bake 45 mins

For the crystallised ginger
120g piece of fresh ginger,
   peeled and cut into
   1cm cubes
200g caster sugar, plus
   2 tbsp for sprinkling

For the parkin
100ml vegetable oil
140g golden syrup
60g black treacle
160g dark muscovado sugar
60g soft pitted prunes,
   finely chopped
25g peeled and finely
   grated fresh ginger
   (prepared weight)
125ml oat milk
200g plain flour
80g fine oatmeal
2 tsp ground ginger
1 tsp ground nutmeg
1 tsp ground cinnamon
¼ tsp ground cloves
¼ tsp fine salt
2 tsp baking powder

For the glacé icing
125g icing sugar,
   plus extra if needed
1 tbsp reserved ginger syrup

YOU WILL NEED
baking sheet lined with
   baking paper
20cm square, loose-bottomed
   cake tin, oiled, then
   lined (base and sides)
   with baking paper

JUDGE'S RECIPE **VEGAN**

Prue's sticky parkin

*Beautifully spiced, parkin is the ultimate in warming, sticky cake –
perfect with a cup of tea on an autumn afternoon, or even better as a
treat on bonfire night, with loved ones huddled together against the chill.*

1. Make the crystallised ginger. Tip the ginger into a small saucepan,
add the 200g of sugar and 200ml of water and bring to the boil. Reduce
the heat and simmer for 30–40 minutes, until soft and translucent.
Pass the ginger through a metal sieve over a heatproof bowl and reserve
the ginger syrup. Spread out the cubes of ginger on the lined baking
sheet and sprinkle with the 2 tablespoons of caster sugar. Place in the
warming drawer or airing cupboard for 30 minutes to dry and crystallise.

2. Heat the oven to 180°C/160°C fan/Gas 4.

3. Make the parkin. Warm the oil, syrup, treacle, muscovado sugar,
prunes and grated ginger in a pan over a low heat, stirring until
combined. Remove the pan from the heat and whisk in the oat milk.

4. Tip the flour, oatmeal, ground ginger, nutmeg, cinnamon, cloves,
salt and baking powder into a large mixing bowl and whisk together
to combine. Make a well in the centre and pour in the syrup mixture.
Whisk slowly, using a balloon whisk, without incorporating any air,
until the mixture is smooth apart from tiny pieces of ginger and prunes.

5. Pour the mixture into the prepared tin and level the top with a palette
knife. Bake it in the middle of the oven for 40–45 minutes, until well
risen and the sponge bounces back when pressed.

6. Remove the parkin from the oven and leave it to cool in the tin on a
wire rack for 10 minutes. Brush with some of the reserved ginger syrup.

7. Make the glacé icing. Sift the icing sugar into a bowl. Add the 1 tablespoon
of reserved ginger syrup and stir until the icing becomes thick enough
to coat the back of a spoon. If necessary, add more ginger syrup to make
the icing runnier, or if the icing becomes too runny, add a spoonful of
additional icing sugar to thicken.

8. Remove the parkin from the tin and transfer it to a wire rack. Spoon
the icing over the cake in a backwards and forwards motion to create
rough diagonal lines. Decorate the top with the crystallised ginger,
then cut into 16 equal squares.

Makes 10
Hands on 30 mins
Bake 50 mins

For the pastry dough
350g plain flour
220g cold vegan unsalted
    butter, cubed
150g ground almonds
120g icing sugar
large pinch of salt
1 tsp vanilla extract
4 tbsp cold water

For the filling
500g frozen forest fruits,
    defrosted and drained
    in a sieve or colander
60g caster sugar
finely grated zest and juice
    of 1 unwaxed lemon
1 tbsp cornflour

YOU WILL NEED
25 x 20cm baking tin,
    lined with baking paper,
    then greased

VEGAN
Forest fruit crumble cookie bars

A perfect dessert on the go – these bars make for a sweet treat in a lunchbox or for a picnic. Or, they would look gorgeous carefully sliced, wrapped in tissue paper and tied with a deep red ribbon as a gift for a neighbour.

1. Heat the oven to 190°C/170°C fan/Gas 5.

2. Make the pastry dough. Put all the ingredients apart from the cold water in a food processor and pulse to a crumb. Gradually, add the water until the mixture forms fine breadcrumbs.

3. Set aside just under half of the pastry crumbs for the crumble topping and tip the remainder into the lined baking tin. Press it out in an even layer, covering the base. Prick the base all over with a fork and bake for 20 minutes, until light golden brown. Leave to cool for 10 minutes.

4. Make the filling. While the pastry base is cooling, toss the forest fruits, sugar, lemon zest and juice and cornflour together. Spread the berry mixture evenly over the cooled pastry.

5. Scatter over the reserved pastry crumbs and return the tin to the oven for another 30 minutes, until the fruit is bubbling, and the crumble topping is golden brown. Leave to cool completely before cutting into 10 equal-sized bars.

Serves 12–16
Hands on 1½ hours + chilling
Bake 30 mins

For the sponges
1 tbsp ground flaxseeds
600g tinned mango purée
250ml plant-based whole milk
190ml vegetable oil
2 tsp vanilla extract
560g plain flour
300g caster sugar
4 tsp baking powder
1½ tsp bicarbonate of soda
½ tsp salt
finely grated zest of
    2 unwaxed limes

For the mango pudding
200g canned mango purée
50g caster sugar
1 tbsp cornflour, mixed
    with 1 tbsp water

For the coconut buttercream
300g unsalted vegan
    butter, softened
1kg icing sugar
170g tinned coconut milk
1 tbsp white rum (optional)
pinch of salt

To decorate
1 small mango, peeled, stone
    removed and cut into slivers
fine curls of lime zest
toasted coconut flakes

YOU WILL NEED
20cm round sandwich tins x 3,
    greased, then base-lined
    with baking paper
large piping bag fitted with
    a medium plain nozzle

VEGAN

Mango and coconut celebration cake

There is sunshine in every slice of this beautiful layer cake. Mango pudding is a traditional Hong Kongese dessert and makes a delicious sweet–tart filling for this tropical-themed showstopper.

1. Heat the oven to 180°C/160°C fan/Gas 4.

2. Make the sponges. Combine the flaxseeds with 3 tablespoons of water in a small bowl and set aside for 10 minutes, until activated and the mixture becomes jelly-like in consistency.

3. In a jug, whisk together the mango purée, plant milk, oil, vanilla and soaked flaxseeds.

4. In a large mixing bowl, sift together the flour, sugar, baking powder, bicarbonate of soda and salt. Stir in the lime zest. Slowly, pour the mango-purée mixture into the bowl, whisking until smooth, and taking care not to overmix.

5. Divide the mixture equally between the lined tins and level the top of each with a palette knife. Bake the sponges on the middle shelves for about 30 minutes, until well risen, golden brown, and a skewer inserted into the centre of each comes out clean. Leave the sponges to cool in the tins for 5 minutes, then turn them out onto a wire rack to cool completely.

6. Make the mango pudding. Heat the mango purée and caster sugar in a small saucepan over a medium heat, stirring until the sugar dissolves. Whisk in the cornflour paste, then bring to the boil. Reduce the heat and simmer, stirring, for 30 seconds, until thickened. Pour the mango pudding into a heatproof container and leave to cool before chilling for about 2 hours – it will thicken further as it cools.

7. Make the coconut buttercream. Beat the butter in a stand mixer fitted with the beater, on medium speed for 2–3 minutes, until pale and fluffy. Reduce the speed slightly and gradually sift in the icing sugar until you have a smooth, thick buttercream. Gradually, pour in the coconut milk and rum (if using), then add the salt, beating for 2 minutes, until smooth. Scoop the buttercream into the large piping bag fitted with the plain nozzle.

Continues overleaf

Free-from **223**

8. Assemble the cake. Put 1 sponge on a cake plate or board. Pipe a 2.5cm border of buttercream around the top edge and fill the middle with half of the mango pudding, spreading it out with a palette knife to cover the centre of the sponge.

9. Pipe 4 lines of buttercream, about 1–2cm thick, over the mango pudding. Place the second sponge on top and repeat with the buttercream and remaining mango pudding. Top with the third sponge.

10. Using a little of the remaining buttercream in the piping bag, cover the assembled cake with a thin layer of buttercream, to crumb coat. Chill for 30 minutes.

11. Use more of the remaining buttercream in the piping bag to add a thick, even layer of buttercream over the top and sides of the cake, spreading it out neatly with a palette knife.

12. Finally, pipe buttercream around the bottom edge and over the top of the cake, then decorate with slivers of fresh mango, a scattering of lime zest, and toasted coconut flakes.

Makes 12
Hands on 50 minutes
+ chilling and resting
Bake 25 mins

For the dough
500g plain flour
60g caster sugar
7g fast-action dried yeast
½ tsp fine salt
300ml plant-based whole milk
   (preferably oat), chilled
75g unsalted vegan butter,
   cubed

For the lamination
300g vegan unsalted butter

For the frangipane
75g unsalted vegan butter,
   softened
90g caster sugar
100g ground almonds
25g plain flour
¼ tsp baking powder
60ml oat milk
½ tbsp almond extract

For the fruit filling
24 tinned apricot halves,
   drained (2 tins)
50g flaked almonds
icing sugar, for dusting

To glaze
1 egg, beaten (for vegan,
   mix 1 tbsp oat milk with
   1 tbsp maple syrup)

YOU WILL NEED
2 baking trays, each lined
   with baking paper

DAIRY-FREE

Apricot and almond Danish pastries

What better way to start the day? These are a sweet, decadent morning treat and perfect with a shot of coffee before heading out to take on the world. Use vegan block butter, rather than a vegan margarine – margarine isn't firm enough for effective lamination in the pastry. Both the dough and the butter need an overnight chill for the best results.

1. Make the dough. Mix the flour, sugar, yeast and salt in a stand mixer fitted with a dough hook on low speed, then gradually add in the milk. When the dough just starts to come together, add the butter and knead on medium–low speed for about 7 minutes, until smooth but slightly sticky. Place the dough in an airtight container and chill it overnight.

2. Grate the butter for lamination on the coarse side of a box grater and chill in the fridge overnight.

3. The next day, dust the work surface with flour and roll out the dough to a 45 x 15cm rectangle. Arrange half of the frozen butter over the bottom two-thirds of the dough, then fold down the top third over the butter and fold up the bottom third, as if folding a letter.

4. Turn the folded dough through 90° and roll it out to a 45 x 15cm rectangle again. Repeat the process, adding the remaining half of frozen butter and folding as before. Place the dough in an airtight container and chill it for 30 minutes.

5. Repeat the rolling and folding process twice more (without any butter), chilling the dough for 30 minutes between each roll and fold.

6. Make the frangipane. Beat the butter and caster sugar in a mixing bowl with a wooden spoon, until creamy, then stir in the ground almonds, flour and baking powder. Gradually stir in the oat milk and add the almond extract, until combined. Set aside while you roll out the dough.

7. Lightly dust the work surface with flour and cut the dough in half. Rewrap one half and return it to the fridge. Roll out the remaining half to a 36 x 24cm rectangle and cut it into six 12cm squares.

Continues overleaf

8. Take one square and, leaving a 1cm border around the edge, spread a tablespoon of the frangipane over the surface. Place two apricot halves, cut side downwards, diagonally across the square. Bring up the exposed corners of the dough, without the apricot halves, to meet over the fruit, and pinch them together to seal. Brush as necessary with a little of the egg (or vegan) glaze, to make the pastry stick together. Transfer the Danish to a lined baking tray.

9. Repeat Step 8 with the remaining squares of dough to make 6 Danish pastries from the first half of the dough. Then, repeat the rolling, cutting, filling and shaping with the remaining half of the dough in the fridge, so that you have 12 Danish pastries in total. Leave the pastries to rest at room temperature for 1 hour.

10. Heat the oven to 200°C/180°C fan/Gas 6.

11. Brush the pastries with a little of the egg wash (or vegan glaze) and scatter over the flaked almonds. Bake for 20–25 minutes, until golden and the pastry is cooked. Transfer to a wire rack and leave to cool completely before dusting with icing sugar to serve.

Serves 8–10
Hands on 45 mins + chilling
Bake 12 mins

For the mousse filling
180g vegan double cream
1 tbsp caster sugar
85g dark chocolate, chopped
½ tsp vanilla extract
pinch of salt

For the sponge
75g plain flour, plus
    extra for dusting
20g cocoa powder
3 large eggs
100g caster sugar,
    plus extra for dusting

For the chocolate glaze
20g cocoa powder
100g icing sugar

YOU WILL NEED
33 x 22cm Swiss roll tin,
    greased, then lined
    with baking paper
    and greased again

DAIRY-FREE

Triple chocolate Swiss roll

This is an indulgent two-tier makeover of the classic chocolate Swiss roll – with added chocolate mousse filling and a chocolate glaze. There is something deeply satisfying about getting that perfect swirl.

1. Heat the oven to 190°C/170°C fan/Gas 5. Scatter a fine dusting of flour and caster sugar over the greased baking paper lining the Swiss roll tin.

2. Make the mousse filling. Gently heat the cream with the caster sugar in a small saucepan until it starts to simmer. Tip the chocolate into a heatproof bowl and carefully pour over the warmed, sweetened cream. Let the chocolate sit for a minute or so before stirring it together with the cream, so that the chocolate melts to a make a glossy ganache.

3. Stir in the vanilla and salt, cover the bowl and chill for 1–2 hours, until completely cold and spreadable.

4. Make the sponge. While the ganache is chilling, sift the flour and cocoa powder together in a mixing bowl. In a separate bowl, use an electric hand whisk to whisk together the eggs and sugar for 3–5 minutes, until thick and mousse-like, and the mixture leaves a ribbon trail when you lift the whisk (alternatively, you can do this in a stand mixer fitted with the whisk attachment, at medium speed).

5. Gently fold the flour and cocoa powder into the egg mixture, until no streaks remain, but working quickly so as not to overmix.

6. Pour the mixture into the prepared tin and carefully spread it out evenly with a palette knife. Bake the sponge on the middle shelf for about 10–12 minutes, until well risen, springy to the touch and starting to pull away from the sides of the tin. Leave to cool for 3–5 minutes.

7. Assemble the Swiss roll. Lay a sheet of baking paper the same size as the sponge on the work surface and sprinkle over an even layer of caster sugar. Carefully invert the sponge onto the sugared paper and peel off the baking paper.

8. Using a small, sharp knife, score a line 2cm from the edge of one of the short ends of the sponge, then carefully roll it up, using the sugared paper to help. Leave the sponge to cool completely.

Continues overleaf

Free-from

9. Once the chocolate mousse is completely chilled, remove it from the fridge and use an electric hand whisk to whisk it for a few minutes until doubled in volume.

10. Unroll the sponge again and spread the whipped chocolate mousse carefully over the surface, leaving a 2cm gap at the short end without the score. Starting from the scored end again, re-roll the sponge up as tightly and neatly as you can. Set it aside.

11. Make the chocolate glaze. Sift the cocoa powder and icing sugar into a bowl, then mix in 2 tablespoons of water, to make a smooth, glossy glaze. Little by little, add up to 1 tablespoon more of water, if needed.

12. Decorate the Swiss roll. Spread the glaze over the outside of the Swiss roll in an even layer. Leave to set and harden for at least 10 minutes before slicing and serving.

Serves 8
Hands on 45 mins + chilling
Bake 40 mins

For the pastry
190g gluten-free plain flour
½ tsp xanthan gum
¼ tsp gluten-free
    baking powder
1 tbsp caster sugar
1 tsp salt
140g unsalted butter,
    cubed and chilled
4–5 tbsp ice-cold water

For the apple filling
600g Braeburn apples,
    peeled, cored and cut
    into thin slices
80g light brown soft sugar
finely grated zest of
    1 unwaxed lemon
juice of ½ lemon
1 tsp ground cinnamon
½ tsp ground ginger
pinch of freshly grated nutmeg
2 tsp cornflour
½ tsp vanilla extract
pinch of salt

For the salted caramel sauce
200g caster sugar
85g unsalted butter
120ml double cream
1 tsp fine salt

To finish
1 egg, lightly beaten
1 tbsp demerara sugar

GLUTEN-FREE

Spiced apple galette

*This is a simple, but brilliant way to use up an abundance of apples –
we've opted for Braeburn here, but any sweet–tart apple will work just
as well, so don't turn away a neighbour who arrives at your door with
armfuls of windfalls. The salted caramel sauce makes it especially indulgent.*

1. Make the pastry. Mix the flour, xanthan gum, baking powder, sugar
and salt in a mixing bowl. Rub in the butter using your fingertips until the
mixture resembles coarse breadcrumbs with large flakes of butter visible.
Gradually, mix in the ice-cold water, stirring until the pastry just starts
to come together in a shaggy and crumbly dough. Flatten the pastry
into a disc, cover and chill for at least 30 minutes.

2. Make the apple filling. In a large clean bowl, mix the apple slices
with the rest of the filling ingredients until evenly combined. Set aside
until the pastry is ready.

3. Heat the oven to 200°C/180°C fan/Gas 6.

4. Assemble and bake the tart. Lightly dust a sheet of baking paper
the same size as your baking tray with flour. Roll out the pastry on the
floured paper to a rough circle, 30–32cm in diameter and about 3mm
thick. The pastry may crumble in places, but just stick it back together.

5. With a slotted spoon, drain the apple slices, leaving the juices in the
bowl, and heap them over the pastry, leaving a 2.5cm border around
the edge. Fold the excess pastry over the edge of the apples, pleating
where necessary. Brush the pastry with the beaten egg and sprinkle
over the demerara sugar. Bake the tart for about 40 minutes, until
the pastry is golden, the apples are soft and the juices bubbling.

6. Make the salted caramel sauce. While the tart is baking, heat the
sugar in a medium pan over a medium heat, stirring occasionally until
it melts to an amber-coloured liquid. Remove the pan from the heat
and carefully add the butter, stirring until melted. If the mixture starts
to separate, use a balloon whisk and whisk until it comes back together.
Return the pan to the heat and slowly pour in the cream, then bring it
to the boil. Reduce the heat and simmer for 1 minute, until thickened
slightly. Remove the pan from the heat, stir in the salt and leave to cool.

7. Cool the baked tart on the tray for 10 minutes, then drizzle with the
salted caramel sauce and serve with ice cream, custard or cream and
any remaining salted caramel sauce in a jug for extra pouring.

Makes 8
Hands on 30 mins + rising and proving
Bake 25 mins

———

200g plant-based whole milk, plus extra for brushing
30g unsalted vegan butter, cubed
350g strong white bread flour
7g fast-action dried yeast
2 tbsp light brown soft sugar
½ tsp ground cinnamon
¼ tsp grated nutmeg
¼ tsp ground ginger
75g sultanas
15g candied peel
vegetable oil, for greasing

YOU WILL NEED
large baking tray lined with baking paper
proving bag

VEGAN
Toasted tea cakes

Put your feet up and sit back with these pillowy classics. Tea cakes remind us of tea shops by the sea, toasted to crunchy on the top and served with lashings of butter. Perfection. Remember to use a vegan butter block, rather than soft vegan margarine, for the best results.

1. Heat the milk and butter in a small pan until the butter just melts, then set aside to cool to lukewarm.

2. Tip the flour, yeast, sugar and spices into a stand mixer fitted with the dough hook and mix to combine. Pour in the lukewarm milk mixture and continue to mix on medium speed to a rough dough. Mix in the sultanas and candied peel.

3. Scrape down the inside of the bowl and knead the dough on medium speed for 5 minutes, until smooth. (Alternatively, mix everything together in a bowl with a wooden spoon, then knead for 7–8 minutes.)

4. Put the dough in a lightly oiled clean mixing bowl, cover with a tea towel and leave to rise in a warm place for about 1–1½ hours, until doubled in size.

5. Roll out the dough on a lightly floured work surface to a 25 x 12cm rectangle (about 2–3cm thick). Cut the rectangle into 8 rough squares and place these spaced out on the lined baking tray. Place in a proving bag and prove in a warm place for 45 minutes, until doubled in size.

6. Heat the oven to 190°C/170°C fan/Gas 5.

7. Brush the top of each tea cake with milk, then bake the tea cakes on the middle shelf for about 25 minutes, until golden brown. Transfer the tea cakes to a wire rack to cool completely.

8. To serve, split each tea cake in half and toast the halves to your liking. Slather in vegan butter.

Conversion Tables

WEIGHT

Metric	Imperial	Metric	Imperial	Metric	Imperial	Metric	Imperial
25g	1oz	200g	7oz	425g	15oz	800g	1lb 12oz
50g	2oz	225g	8oz	450g	1lb	850g	1lb 14oz
75g	2½oz	250g	9oz	500g	1lb 2oz	900g	2lb
85g	3oz	280g	10oz	550g	1lb 4oz	950g	2lb 2oz
100g	4oz	300g	11oz	600g	1lb 5oz	1kg	2lb 4oz
125g	4½oz	350g	12oz	650g	1lb 7oz		
140g	5oz	375g	13oz	700g	1lb 9oz		
175g	6oz	400g	14oz	750g	1lb 10oz		

VOLUME

Metric	Imperial	Metric	Imperial	Metric	Imperial	Metric	Imperial
30ml	1fl oz	150ml	¼ pint	300ml	½ pint	500ml	18fl oz
50ml	2fl oz	175ml	6fl oz	350ml	12fl oz	600ml	1 pint
75ml	2½fl oz	200ml	7fl oz	400ml	14fl oz	700ml	1¼ pints
100ml	3½fl oz	225ml	8fl oz	425ml	⅔ pint	850ml	1½ pints
125ml	4fl oz	250ml	9fl oz	450ml	16fl oz	1 litre	1¾ pints

LINEAR

Metric	Imperial	Metric	Imperial	Metric	Imperial	Metric	Imperial
5mm	¼in	6cm	2½in	11cm	4¼in	18cm	7in
1cm	½in	7cm	2¾in	12cm	4½in	20cm	8in
2.5cm	1in	7.5cm	3in	13cm	5in	21cm	8¼in
3cm	1¼in	8cm	3¼in	14cm	5½in	22cm	8½in
4cm	1½in	9cm	3½in	15cm	6in	23cm	9in
5cm	2in	9.5cm	3¾in	16cm	6¼in	24cm	9½in
5.5cm	2¼in	10cm	4in	17cm	6½in	25cm	10in

US CUP

Ingredients	1 cup	¾ cup	⅔ cup	½ cup	⅓ cup	¼ cup	2 tbsp
Brown sugar	180g	135g	120g	90g	60g	45g	23g
Butter	240g	180g	160g	120g	80g	60g	30g
Cornflour (cornstarch)	120g	90g	80g	60g	40g	30g	15g
Flour	120g	90g	80g	60g	40g	30g	15g
Icing sugar (powdered/confectioners')	100g	75g	70g	50g	35g	25g	13g
Nuts (chopped)	150g	110g	100g	75g	50g	40g	20g
Nuts (ground)	120g	90g	80g	60g	40g	30g	15g
Oats	90g	65g	60g	45g	30g	22g	11g
Raspberries	120g	90g	80g	60g	40g	30g	--
Salt	300g	230g	200g	150g	100g	75g	40g
Sugar (caster/superfine)	225g	170g	150g	115g	75g	55g	30g
Sugar (granulated)	200g	150g	130g	100g	65g	50g	25g
Sultanas/raisins	200g	150g	130g	100g	65g	50g	22g
Water/milk	250ml	180ml	150ml	120ml	75ml	60ml	30ml

SPOON MEASURES

Metric	Imperial
5ml	1 tsp
10ml	2 tsp
15ml	1 tbsp
30ml	2 tbsp
45ml	3 tbsp
60ml	4 tbsp
75ml	5 tbsp

OVEN TEMPERATURES

°C	°F	Gas	°C	°F	Gas
70	150	¼	180	350	4
100	200	½	190	375	5
110	225	½	200	400	6
130	250	1	210	415	6–7
140	275	1	220	425	7
150	300	2	230	450	8
160	315	2–3	240	475	8
170	325	3	250	500	9

Inspire me...

Use this visual index when you need inspiration for a bake to offer comfort in a particular way. For example, *Duvet Days* lists those bakes that we hope will wrap you in a feeling of wellness when you're under par. *Nostalgia* features bakes that transport you to a happy memory. Look to *Sending Love* for bakes that are perfect for gifting, to bring the comfort of kindness to someone in need. Try the bakes in *Rainy Days* when the weather makes you want to hunker down in your kitchen. The bakes in *Lose Yourself* are good when you need to immerse yourself fully in the process – kneading, rolling, folding, decorating – to switch off from the world. *Surrounded by Love* offers bakes for feeding a crowd, when comfort comes in gathering together those you love. Finally, try the bakes in *By the Fireside* for days when you just want to be in cosy socks next to a roaring fire.

Duvet days

Fruit Slice Traybake (p.42)

Mini Victoria Sandwiches (p.46)

Date and Pistachio Flapjacks (p.50)

Seeded Bloomer (p.72)

Orange and Salted Caramel Doughnuts (p.75)

Savoury Crumpets (p.83)

Iced Cinnamon Rolls (p.89)

Cornbread (p.92)

Blackberry, Blueberry and Custard Brioche Buns (p.131)

Pastéis de Nata (p.133)

Mac 'n' Cheese Danish Pastries (p.153)

Prue's Spotted Dick and Custard (p.163)

Panettone Bread and Butter Pudding (p.178)

Apple and Blackberry Crumble Pie (p.184)

Chocolate Skillet Cake (p.194)

Cherry and Almond Blondies (p.201)

Triple Chocolate Muffins (p.202)

Banana and Chocolate Marble Cake (p.207)

Turtle Bars (p.210)

Raspberry and Coconut Traybake (gf) (p.217)

Prue's Sticky Parkin (vg) (p.218)

Forest Fruit Crumble Cookie Bars (vg) (p.220)

Apricot and Almond Danish Pastries (df) (p.225)

Toasted Tea Cakes (vg) (p.234)

Nostalgia

Paul's Mini Battenbergs (p.27)

Coffee and Walnut Lambeth Cake (p.35)

Fruit Slice Traybake (p.42)

Mini Victoria Sandwiches (p.46)

Prue's Mint Chocolate Biscuits (p.59)

Fresh Cream Iced Buns (p.80)

Fruit Scones (p.90)

Cornish Pasties (p.96)

Cherry Bakewell Tarts (p.111)

Mum's Cheese and Onion Pie (p.116)

Steak and Kidney Pudding (p.123)

Summer Berry Jam Crostata (p.125)

Pastéis de Nata (p.133)

Prue's Pear Tarte Tatin (p.137)

Summer Berry Sheet Pavlova (p.160)

Prue's Spotted Dick and Custard (p.163)

Mince Pies (p.169)

Paul's Banoffee Pie (p.175)

Panettone Bread and Butter Pudding (p.178)

Salted Caramel Self-saucing Puddings (p.182)

Raspberry and Coconut Traybake (gf) (p.217)

Prue's Sticky Parkin (vg) (p.218)

Triple Chocolate Swiss Roll (df) (p.229)

Toasted Tea Cakes (vg) (p.234)

Sending love

Rhubarb Upside-down Cake with Custard (p.24)

Paul's Mini Battenbergs (p.27)

Fruit Slice Traybake (p.42)

Mini Victoria Sandwiches (p.46)

Date and Pistachio Flapjacks (p.50)

Brown Butter, Coffee and Cinnamon Chocolate Chip Cookies (p.52)

Butterscotch and Pecan Shortbread Biscuits (p.56)

Prue's Mint Chocolate Biscuits (p.59)

Boozy Viennese Fingers (p.54)

Hunters' Buttons (p.65)

Golden Syrup Cookies (p.66)

Fruit Scones (p.90)

Friday Night Curry Pies (p.101)

Med Veg Puff Tart (p.107)

Cherry Bakewell Tarts (p.111)

Prosciutto, Taleggio and Fig Twists (p.119)

242 *Inspire me...*

Pastéis de Nata (p.133)

Chocolate Madeleines (p.141)

Spiced Butternut Pie with Maple Pecan Streusel (p.147)

Mince Pies (p.169)

Chocolate Orange Babka Knots (p.197)

Cherry and Almond Blondies (p.201)

Triple Chocolate Muffins (p.202)

Banana and Chocolate Marble Cake (p.207)

Turtle Bars (p.210)

Confit Garlic, Olive and Rosemary Focaccia (gf) (p.214)

Raspberry and Coconut Traybake (gf) (p.217)

Forest Fruit Crumble Cookie Bars (vg) (p.220)

Rainy days

Lemon Meringue Cake (p.29)

Coffee and Walnut Lambeth Cake (p.35)

Brown Butter, Coffee and Cinnamon Chocolate Chip Cookies (p.52)

Boozy Viennese Fingers (p.54)

Prue's Mint Chocolate Biscuits (p.59)

Iced Bug Biscuits (p.61)

Orange and Salted Caramel Doughnuts (p.75)

Fresh Cream Iced Buns (p.80)

Paul's Spanakopita (p.99)

Almond Bear Claws (p.113)

Summer Berry Jam Crostata (p.125)

Blackberry, Blueberry and Custard Brioche Buns (p.131)

Prue's Pear Tarte Tatin (p.137)

Chocolate Madeleines (p.141)

Fig and Raspberry Tarts with Burnt Honey Cream (p.143)

Mac 'n' Cheese Danish Pastries (p.153)

Roasted Plum Brown-sugar
Meringues (p.156)

Baklava Cheesecake (p.171)

Key Lime Pie (p.181)

Malted Chocolate and
Honeycomb Layer Cake (p.189)

Chocolate and Hazelnut
Mini Cakes (p.191)

Chocolate Skillet Cake
(p.194)

Confit Garlic, Olive and
Rosemary Focaccia (gf) (p.214)

Forest Fruit Crumble Cookie
Bars (vg) (p.220)

Lose yourself

Brown Sugar and Spice Cake (p.21)

Rhubarb Upside-down Cake with Custard (p.24)

Lemon Meringue Cake (p.29)

Coffee and Walnut Lambeth Cake (p.35)

Pistachio, Raspberry and Vanilla Cake (p.39)

Boozy Viennese Fingers (p.54)

Iced Bug Biscuits (p.61)

Paul's Seven-strand Plaited Wreath (p.86)

Iced Cinnamon Rolls (p.89)

Paul's Spanakopita (p.99)

Dutch Apple Pie (p.105)

Med Veg Puff Tart (p.107)

Almond Bear Claws (p.113)

Summer Berry Jam Crostata (p.125)

Blackberry, Blueberry and Custard Brioche Buns (p.131)

Pastéis de Nata (p.133)

Inspire me...

Fig and Raspberry Tarts with Burnt Honey Cream (p.143)

'Fallen Angel' Profiteroles (p.149)

Lemon and Passion Fruit Brûlée Tart (p.165)

Malted Chocolate and Honeycomb Layer Cake (p.189)

Chocolate Orange Babka Knots (p.197)

Apricot, Ginger and Almond Chocolate Mousse Cake (p.205)

Confit Garlic, Olive and Rosemary Focaccia (gf) (p.214)

Apricot and Almond Danish Pastries (df) (p.225)

Surrounded by love

Brown Sugar and Spice Cake (p.21)

Rhubarb Upside-down Cake with Custard (p.24)

Lemon Meringue Cake (p.29)

Carrot and Pumpkin Cake (p.32)

Coffee and Walnut Lambeth Cake (p.35)

Pistachio, Raspberry and Vanilla Cake (p.39)

Mochamisu Layer Cake (p.45)

Fruit and Nut Crackers (p.68)

Calabrese Sourdough Pizza (p.77)

Paul's Spanakopita (p.99)

Friday Night Curry Pies (p.101)

Dutch Apple Pie (p.105)

Med Veg Puff Tart (p.107)

Mum's Cheese and Onion Pie (p.116)

Prosciutto, Taleggio and Fig Twists (p.119)

Blackberry, Blueberry and Custard Brioche Buns (p.131)

Spiced Butternut Pie with Maple Pecan Streusel (p.147)

'Fallen Angel' Profiteroles (p.149)

Roasted Plum Brown-sugar Meringues (p.156)

Summer Berry Sheet Pavlova (p.160)

Prue's Spotted Dick and Custard (p.163)

Lemon and Passion Fruit Brûlée Tart (p.165)

Baklava Cheesecake (p.171)

Paul's Banoffee Pie (p.175)

Panettone Bread and Butter Pudding (p.178)

Apple and Blackberry Crumble Pie (p.184)

Malted Chocolate and Honeycomb Layer Cake (p.189)

Chocolate Skillet Cake (p.194)

Apricot, Ginger and Almond Chocolate Mousse Cake (p.205)

Confit Garlic, Olive and Rosemary Focaccia (gf) (p.214)

Mango and Coconut Celebration Cake (vg) (p.223)

Spiced Apple Galette (gf) (p.233)

By the fireside

Fruit Slice Traybake (p.42)

Butterscotch and Pecan Shortbread Biscuits (p.56)

Golden Syrup Cookies (p.66)

Fruit and Nut Crackers (p.68)

Seeded Bloomer (p.72)

Orange and Salted Caramel Doughnuts (p.75)

Savoury Crumpets (p.83)

Cornbread (p.92)

Friday Night Curry Pies (p.101)

Prosciutto, Taleggio and Fig Twists (p.119)

Summer Berry Jam Crostata (p.125)

Pastéis de Nata (p.133)

Mac 'n' Cheese Danish Pastries (p.153)

Mince Pies (p.169)

Salted Caramel Self-saucing Puddings (p.182)

Chocolate and Hazelnut Mini Cakes (p.191)

Chocolate Orange Babka
Knots (p.197)

Cherry and Almond
Blondies (p.201)

Triple Chocolate Muffins
(p.202)

Banana and Chocolate
Marble Cake (p.207)

Turtle Bars (p.210)

Prue's Sticky Parkin (vg)
(p.218)

Spiced Apple Galette (gf)
(p.233)

Toasted Tea Cakes (vg)
(p.234)

Index

This book is published to accompany the television series entitled The Great British Baking Show, broadcast on Channel 4 in 2024

The Great British Baking Show® is a registered trademark of Love Productions Ltd

Series produced for Channel 4 Television by Love Productions

The Great British Baking Show: Comfort Bakes

First published in The United States in 2024 by Sphere

10 9 8 7 6 5 4 3 2 1

A CIP catalogue record for this book is available from the British Library.

ISBN: 9781408734063

New recipes developed and written by Annie Rigg

Senior Commissioning Editor: Tig Wallace
Design & Art Direction: Smith & Gilmour
Project Editor: Judy Barratt
Copyeditor: Nicola Graimes
Food Photographer: Ant Duncan
Assistant Food Photographers: Jonathan Leigh and Sam Milton
On-set Photographer: Smith & Gilmour
Baker Portrait Photographer: Mark Bourdillon
Food Stylist: Annie Rigg
Assistant Food Stylists: Hattie Baker, Lara Cook, Samantha Duff and Laura Urschel
Props Stylist: Hannah Wilkinson
Production Manager: Abby Marshall
Cover Design: Smith & Gilmour

Publisher's thanks to: Joff, Suzie, Sidney and Ralph Adams; Hilary Bird; Hugh Dowdall; Sarah Epton; Krystal and Amelie Houston; Ifrah Ismail; Lily and Oscar Smith; Victoria Onions; Scarlett Wilson

Typeset in Recoleta, Goldney and Kievit Pro
Colour origination by Born Group
Printed and bound in Canada by Friesens Corporation

Papers used by Sphere are from well-managed forest and other responsible sources.

Sphere
An imprint of Little, Brown Book Group, Carmelite House, 50 Victoria Embankment, London EC4Y 0DZ
An Hachette UK Company
www.hachette.co.uk www.littlebrown.co.uk

WITH THANKS

Love Productions would like to thank the following people:
Executive Producer: Jenna Mansfield
Food & Challenge Producer: Katy Bigley
Home Economist: Becca Watson
Love Executives: Letty Kavanagh, Rupert Frisby, Kieran Smith, Joe Bartley
Publicists: Amanda Console, Shelagh Pymm
Commissioning Editor: Vivienne Molokwu

Thank you also to: Paul, Prue, Noel and Alison. *And to the bakers for their recipes:*
Andy, Christiaan, Dylan, Georgie, Gill, Hazel, Illiyin, Jeff, John, Mike, Nelly and Sumayah.